Joseph
HAYDN
TWO HORN CONCERTOS
H.VIId:3-4
Edited by
Clark McAlister

Study Score
Partitur

SERENISSIMA MUSIC, INC.

PREFACE

The two concertos presented here were once thought to have represented a pair of 'bookends' for Joseph Haydn's wind concerto output. This notion has since been cast into doubt due to the fact that the second concerto is now considered spurious by most Haydn scholars and moreover likely dates from the same decade as the first concerto, whose authenticty is fortunately affirmed thanks to the composer's own manuscript, which exists to this day and was even published in facsimile in 2009.

The first concerto, listed as VIId:3 in Hoboken's catalogue, was composed in 1762 in the first or second year of Haydn's long tenure of service to the Esterházy court. In the later part of 1761 Haydn was busy hiring players for the court orchestra of Prince Paul Anton Esterházy. For principal horn, he engaged Thaddaus Steinmüller (1725-1790) who was famous for his mastery of the instruments high and middle register, which coincides with the overall tessitura of the solo part. While Steinmüller is the most obvious choice of soloist for the concerto's presumed premiere in either 1762 or 1763, another theory argues the concerto was composed for the baptism of a child of the hornist Joseph Leutgeb (1732-1811), most famous for his connection with the horn concertos of Mozart.

In any case, the composer's manuscript remains in existence to this day, housed in the famous collection of Vienna's Gessellschaft der Musikfreunde. The work remained unpublished until 1898 when Breitkopf und Härtel issued an edition prepared by Euseubius Mandyczewski. The sources for the present edition are the composer's manuscript and Mandyczewski's first edition.

The second concerto here was also published in 1898 in an edition by Mandyczewski. This was not the first publication of the concerto though, for it is listed in the 1781 Supplement of the Breitkopf catalogue as being available in manuscript copies. Hoboken's catalog from 1957 lists it as VIId:4, though he mentions the question of authenticy. The only documented contemporary manuscript at the time of the present edition is the one located in the Christian-Weise-Bibliothek in Zwittau, Saxony. Mandyczdewski produced a score from the Zwittau parts in advance of his 1898 publication. Subsequent research has raised considerable doubt about Joseph Haydn's authorship and has dated the work to around 1767. In an article published in 1968 the Haydn scholar H. C. Robbins-Landon advanced the theory that this concerto is likely the work of Joseph Haydn's younger brother Michael.

The Zwittau manuscript parts being unavailable in 1994, the present edition is therefore based upon the score prepared by Eusebius Mandyczewski from the Zwittau material and the 1898 Breitkopf edition. For practical reasons, Mandyczewski seems to have added 11 bars to the third movement between measure 143 and the cadenza-fermata at bar 154. An optional cut is marked for the added measures (possibly in another hand), which has been retained in the present score.

The Editor

ORCHESTRA

Concerto No.1, Hob.VIId.3

2 Oboes

Solo Horn (D)

Violin I

Violin II

Viola

Violoncello

Double Bass

Duration: ca.14 minutes

Composed 1762
First presumed performance: 1762 or 1763
Esterhazy Castle
Thaddaus Steinmüller (horn)
Esterhazy Orchestra, Joseph Haydn (director)

Concerto No.2, Hob.VIId.4

Solo Horn (D)

Violin I

Violin II

Viola

Violoncello

Double Bass

Duration: ca.16 minutes

Composed ca.1767, Published in Breitkopf calaogue, 1781
First performance: Unknown
Authenticity doubtful. Possibly the work of Michael Haydn

ISMN: 978-1-60874-277-6

Concerto (No. 1)

for Horn and Orchestra

I

Joseph Haydn (H. VIId:3)
Edited by Clark McAlister

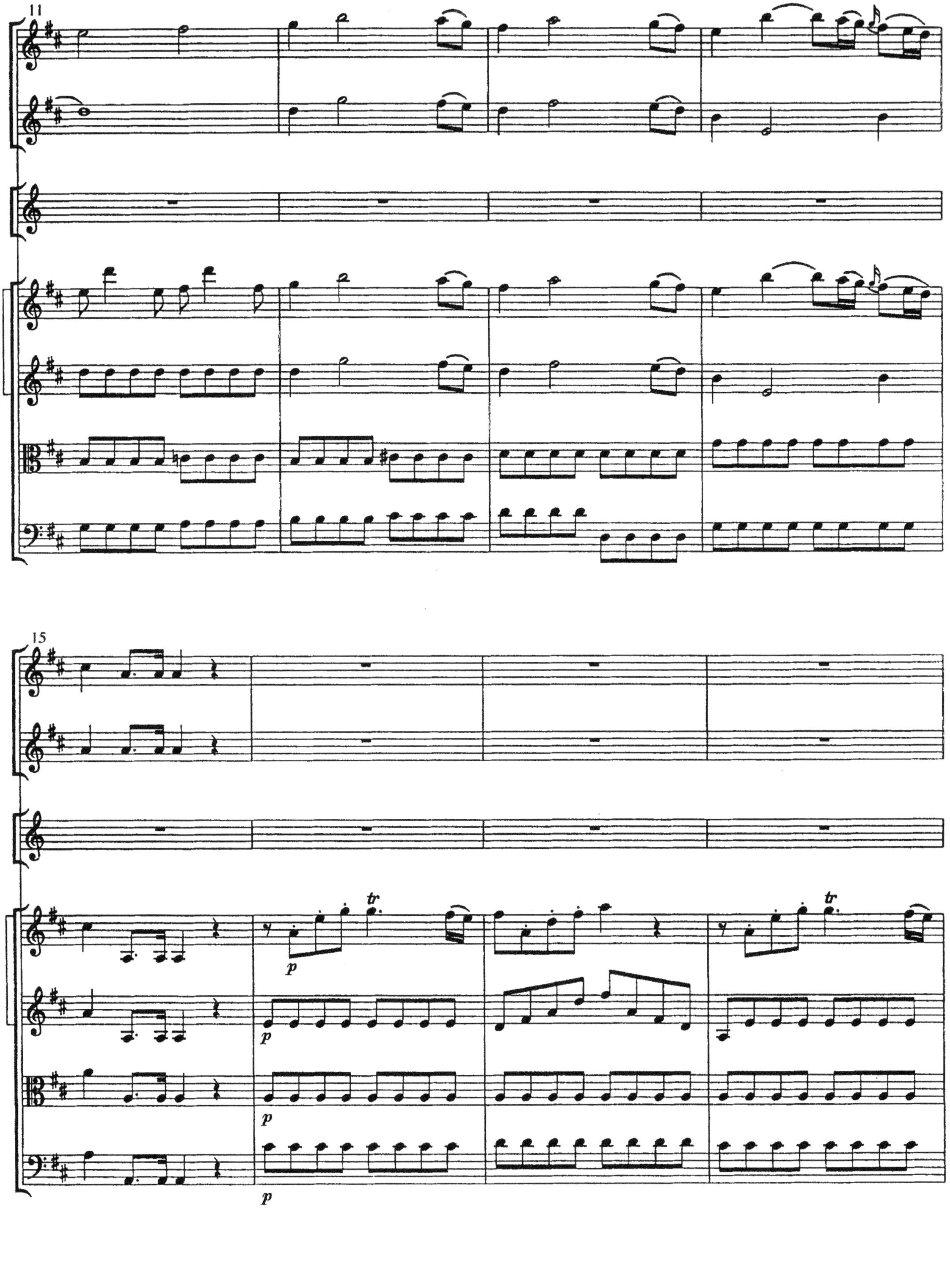
11
15
tr
p

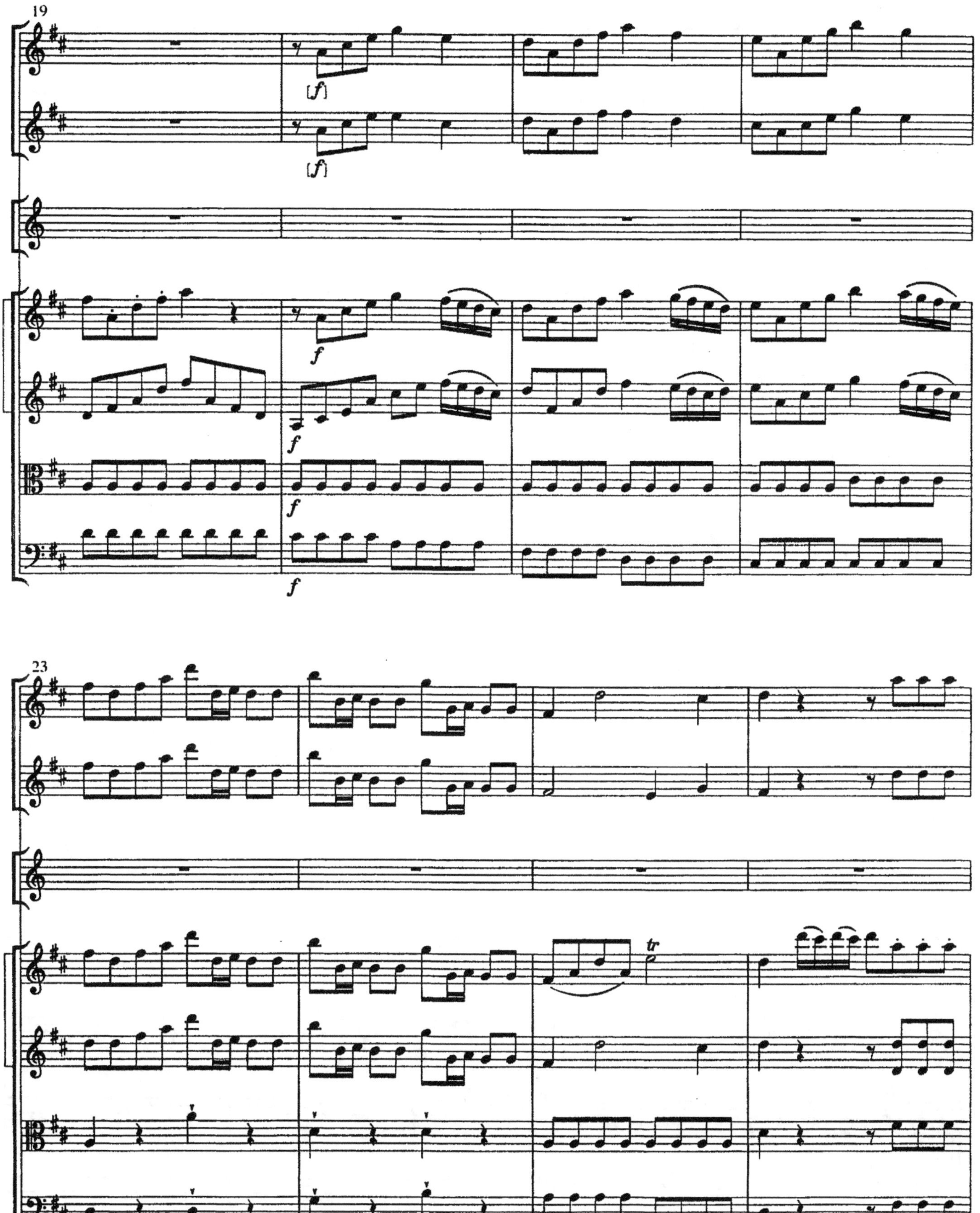
19
[f]
[f]
f
f
f
f
23
tr

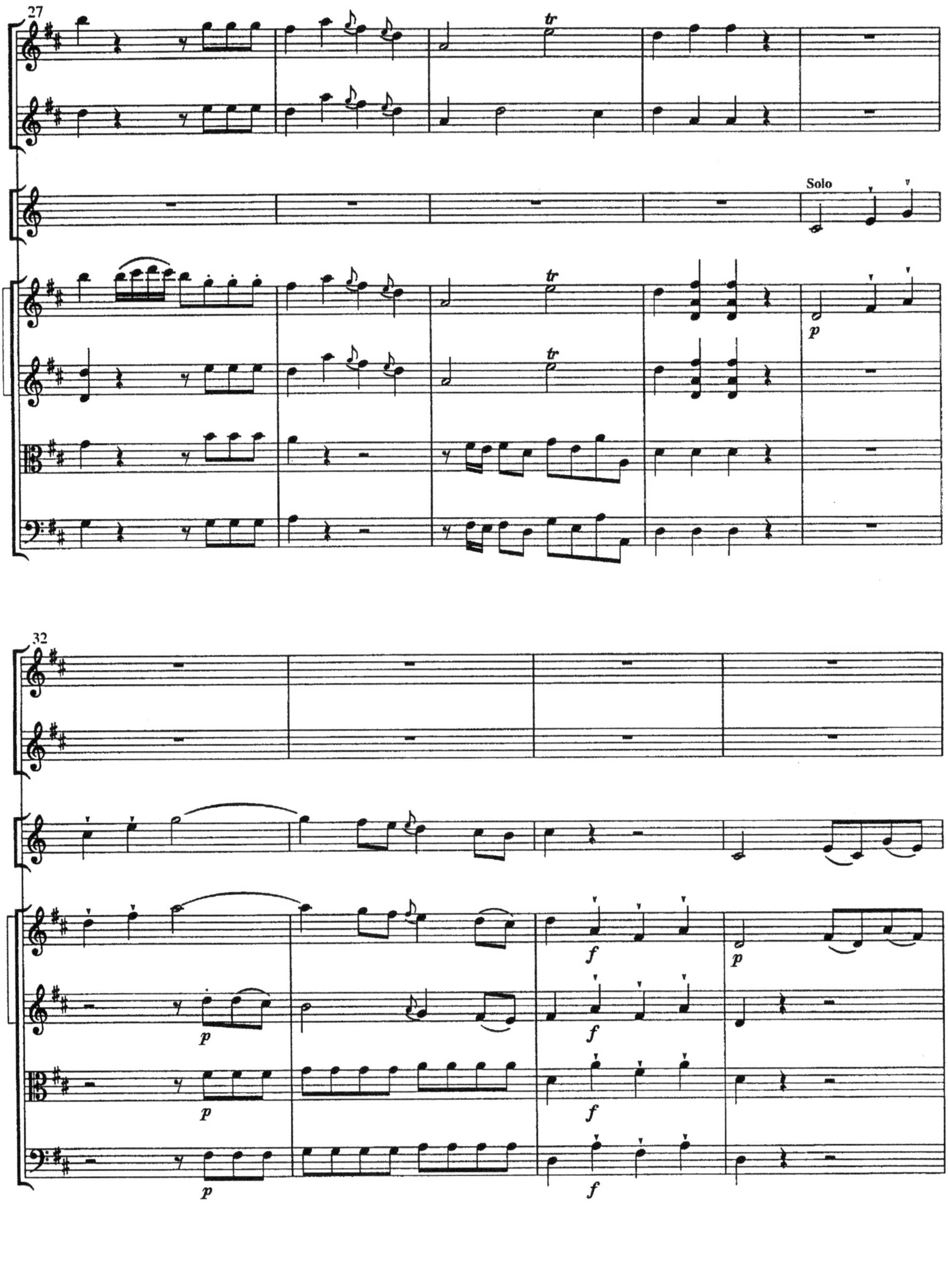
27
tr
Solo
tr
tr
32
p
f
p
p
f
p
f
p
f

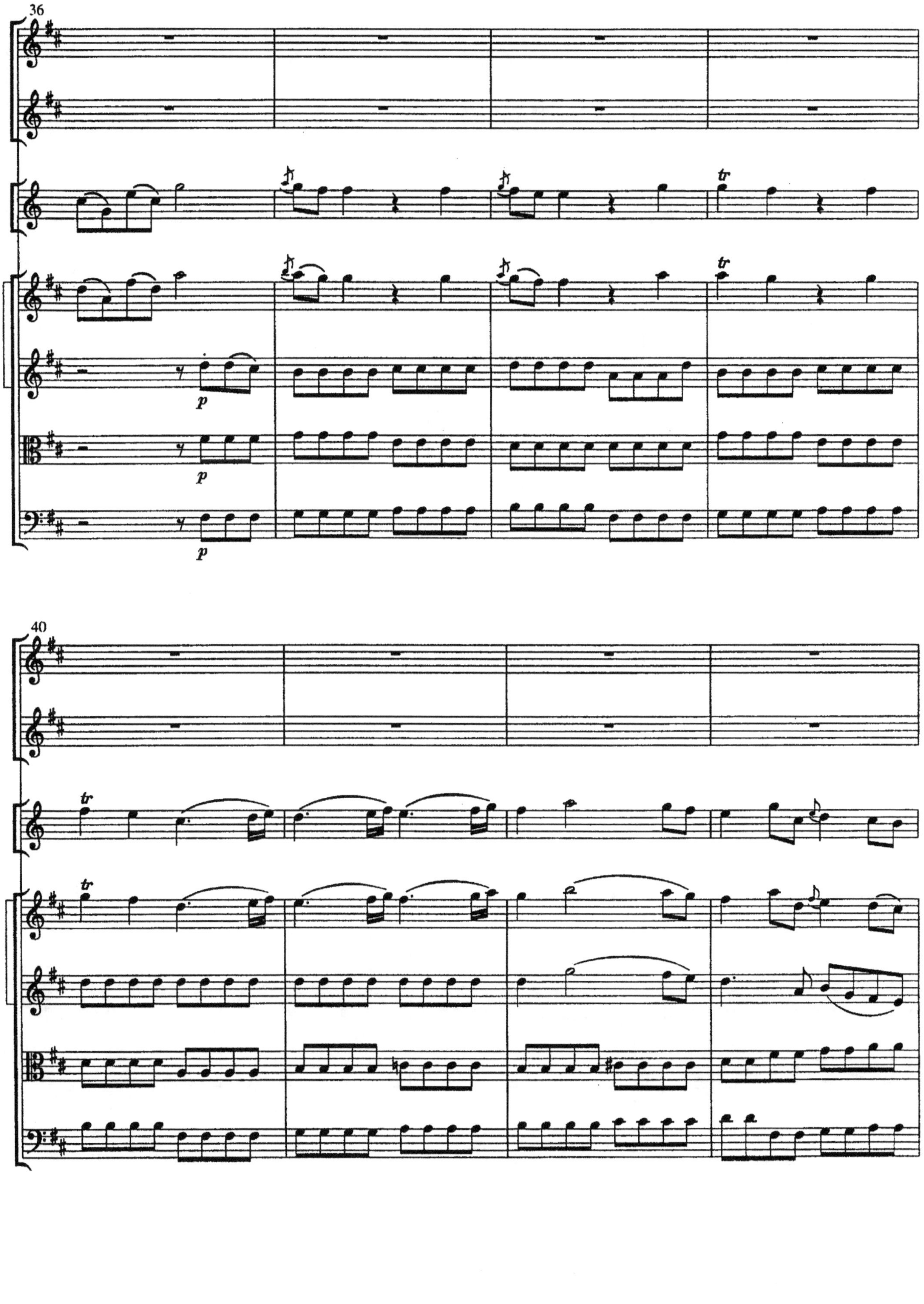
36
tr
p
40
tr

6

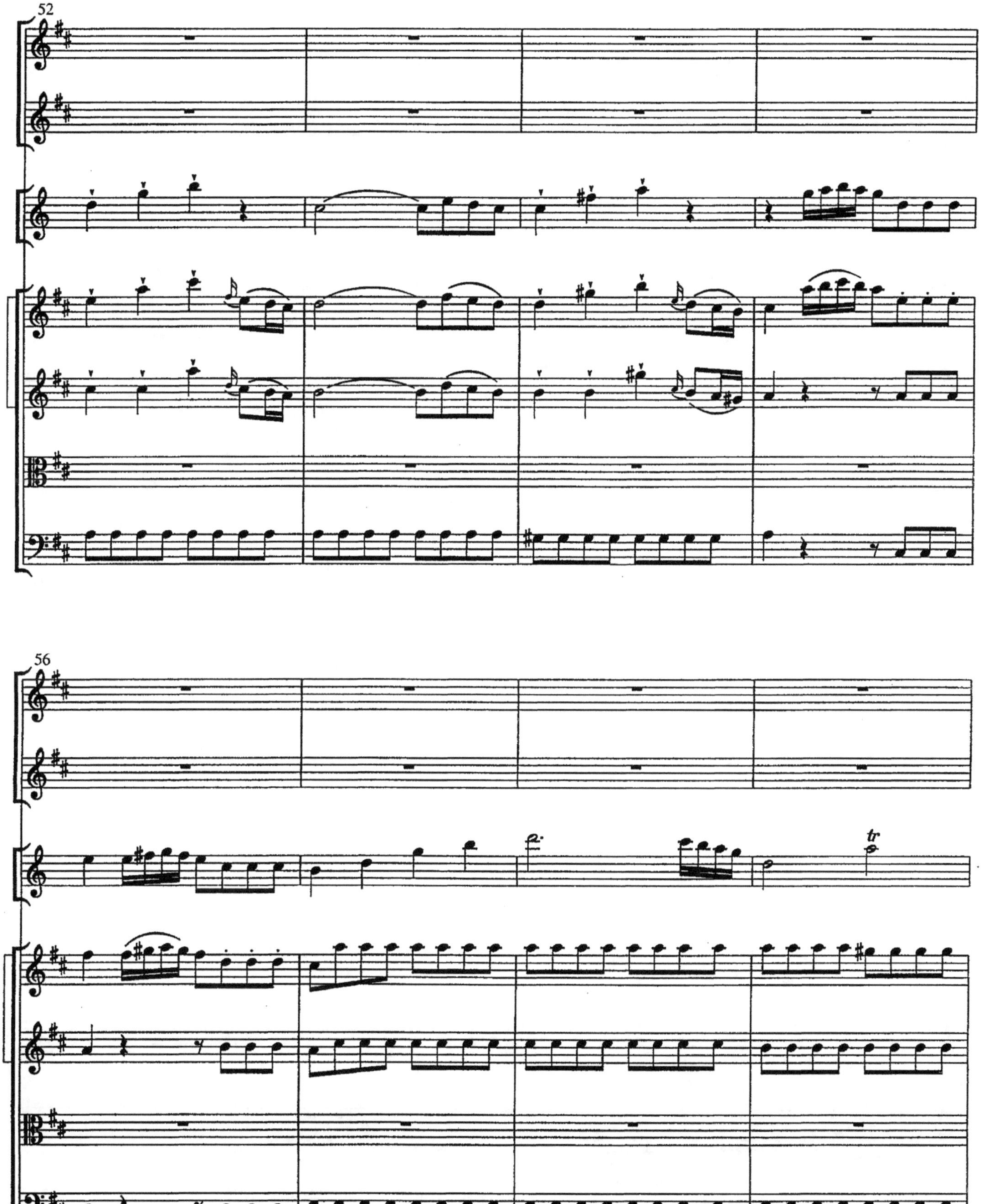
52
56
tr

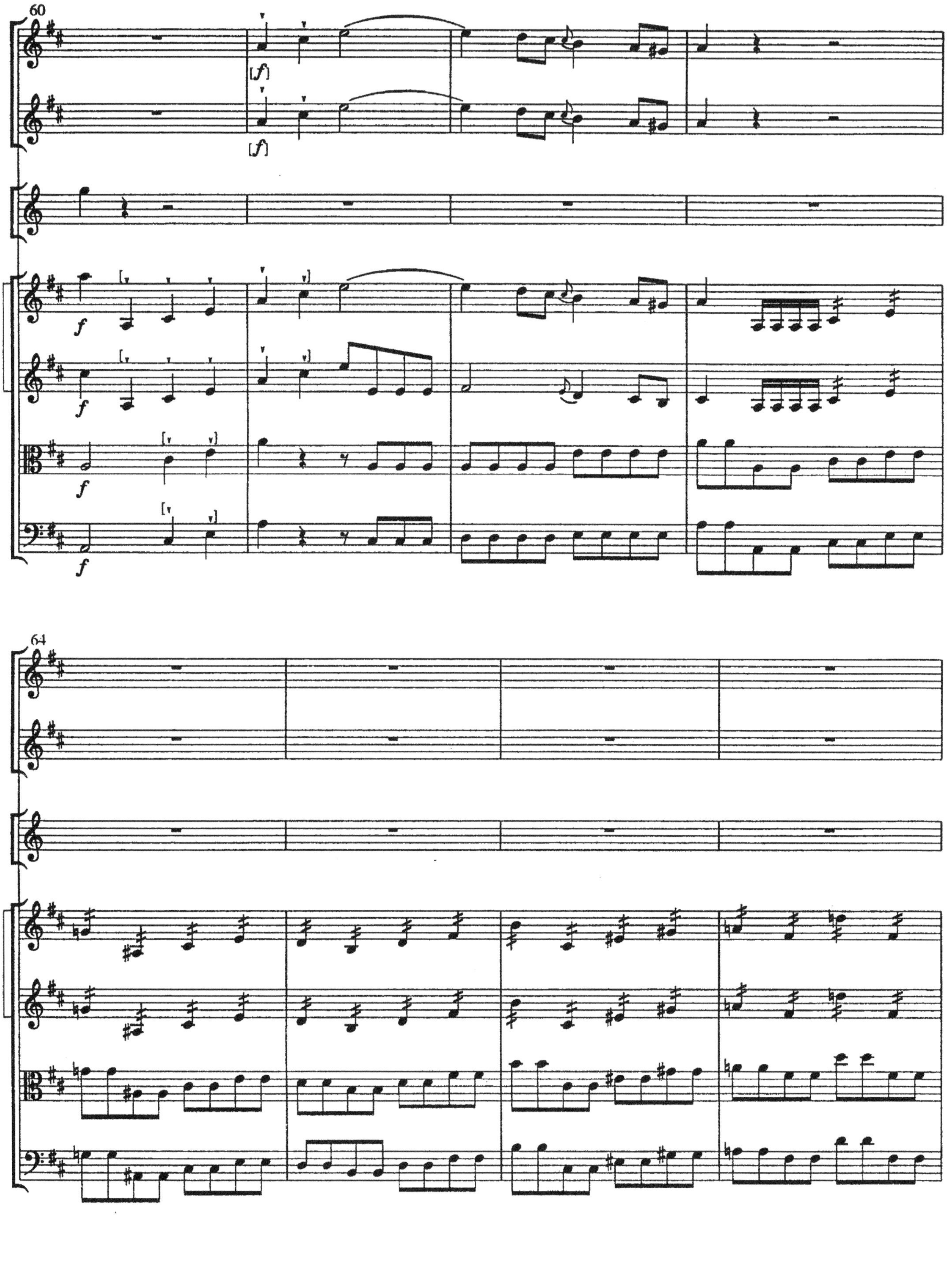
60
[f]
[f]
f
f
f
f
64

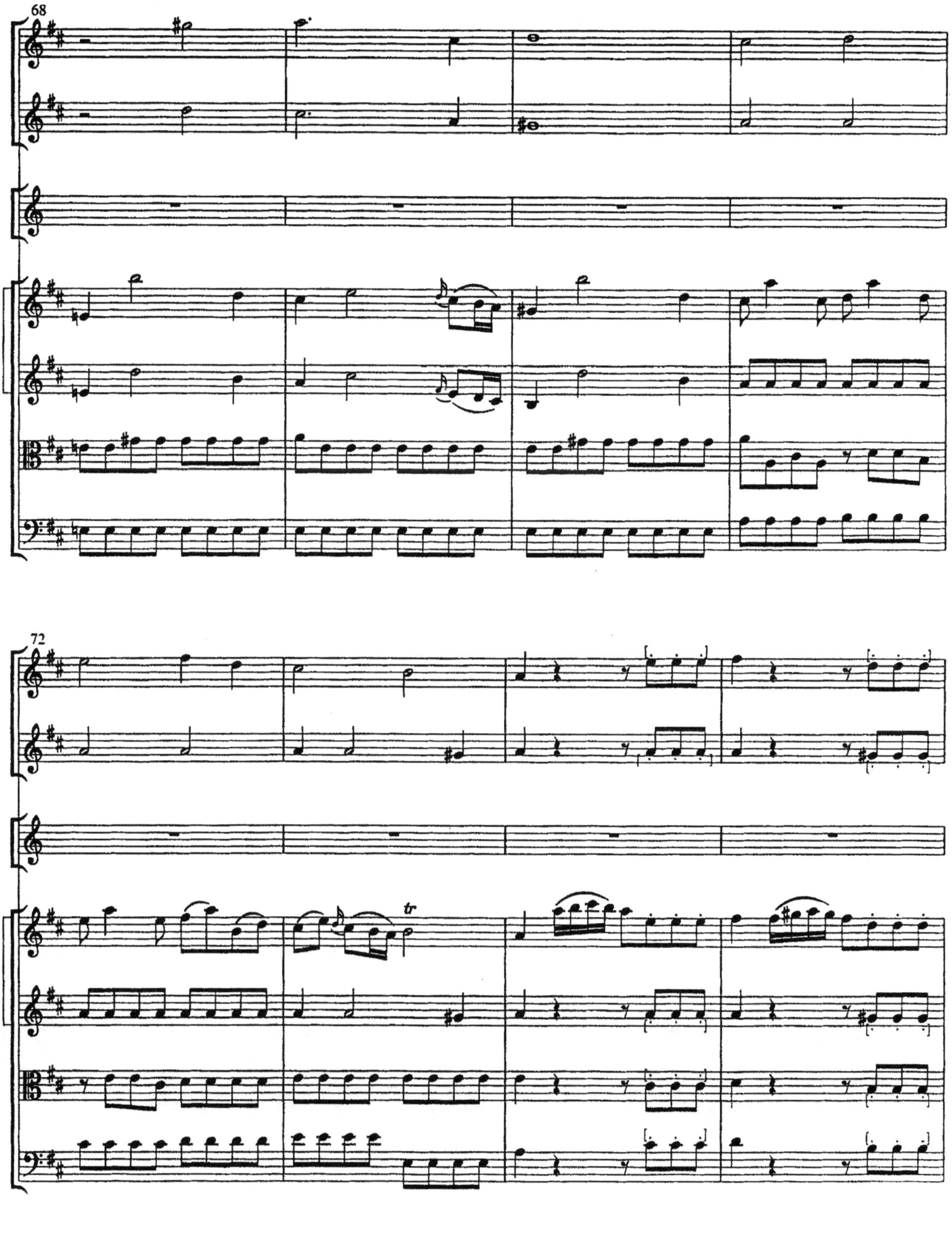
68
72
tr

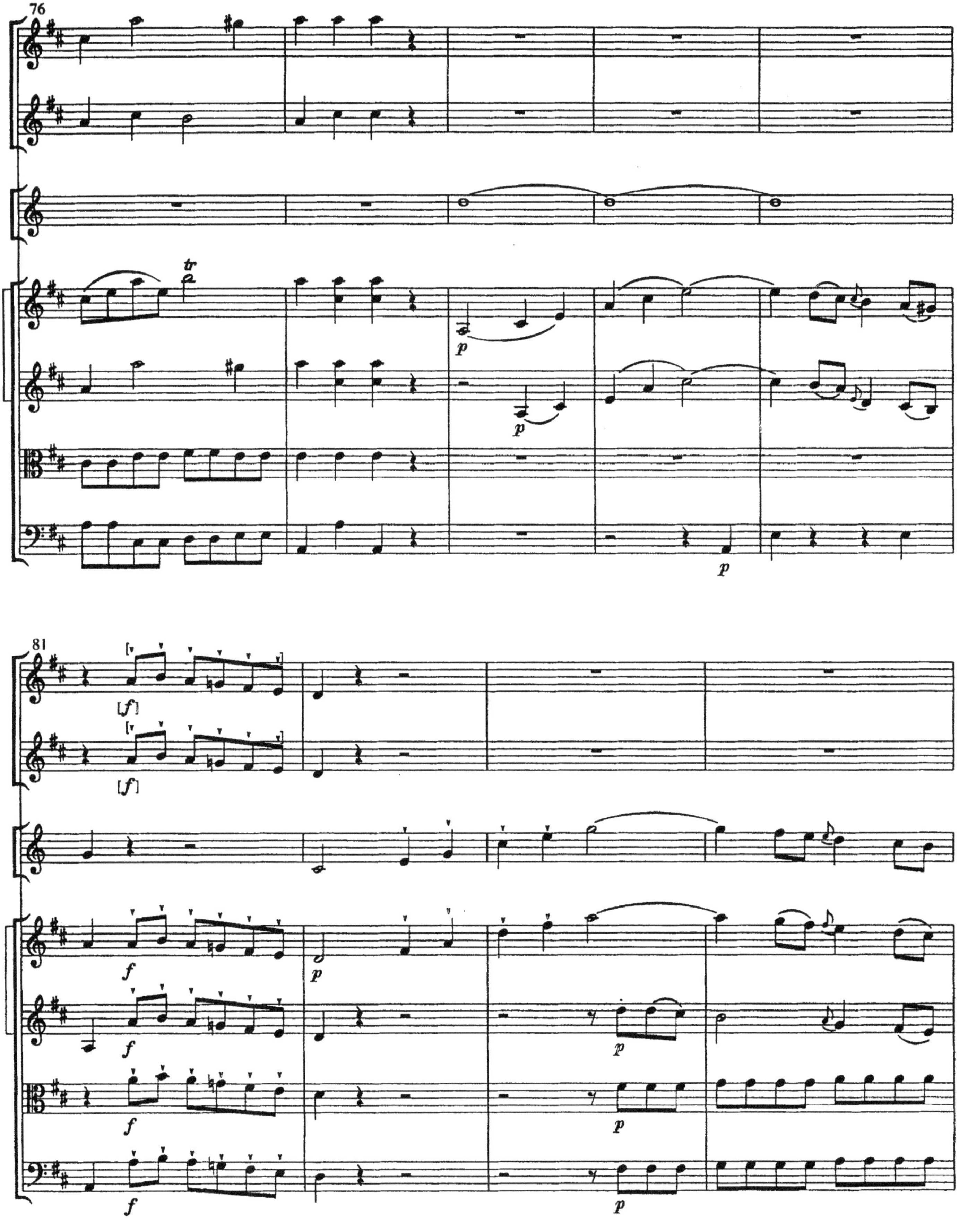
76
tr
p
p
p
81
[f]
[f]
f
p
f
p
f
p
f
p

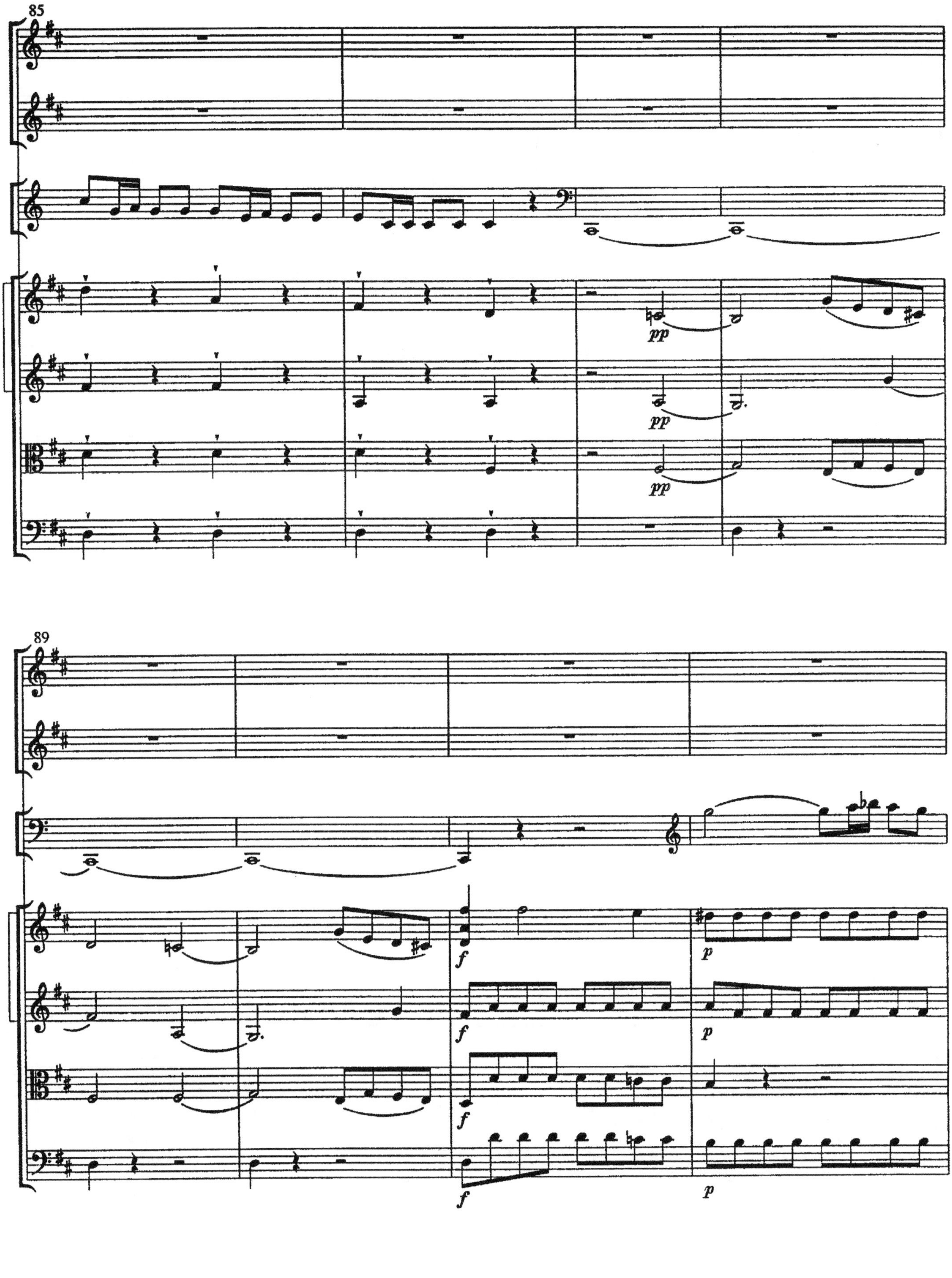
85
89

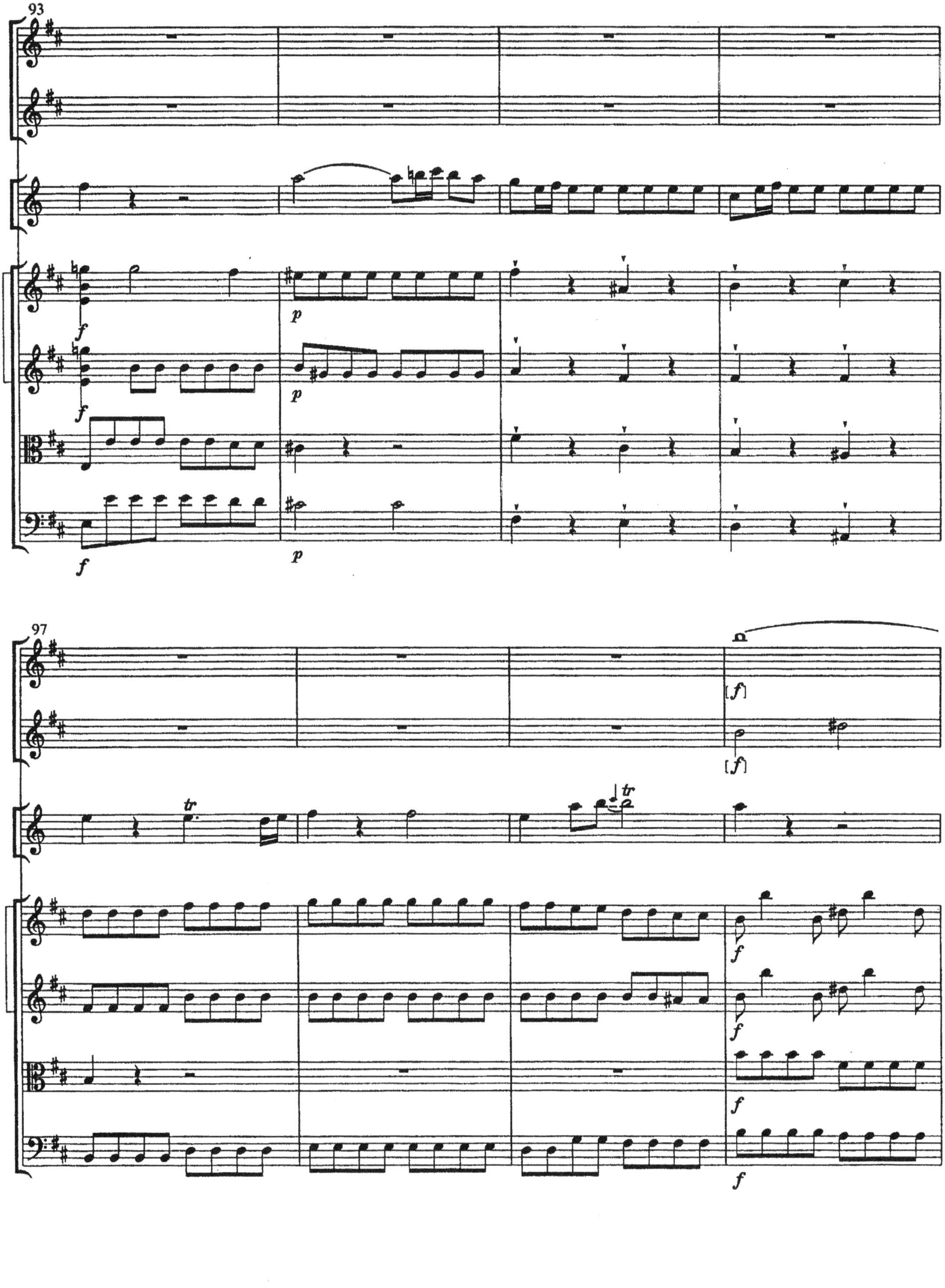
93
f
p
97
tr
[f]

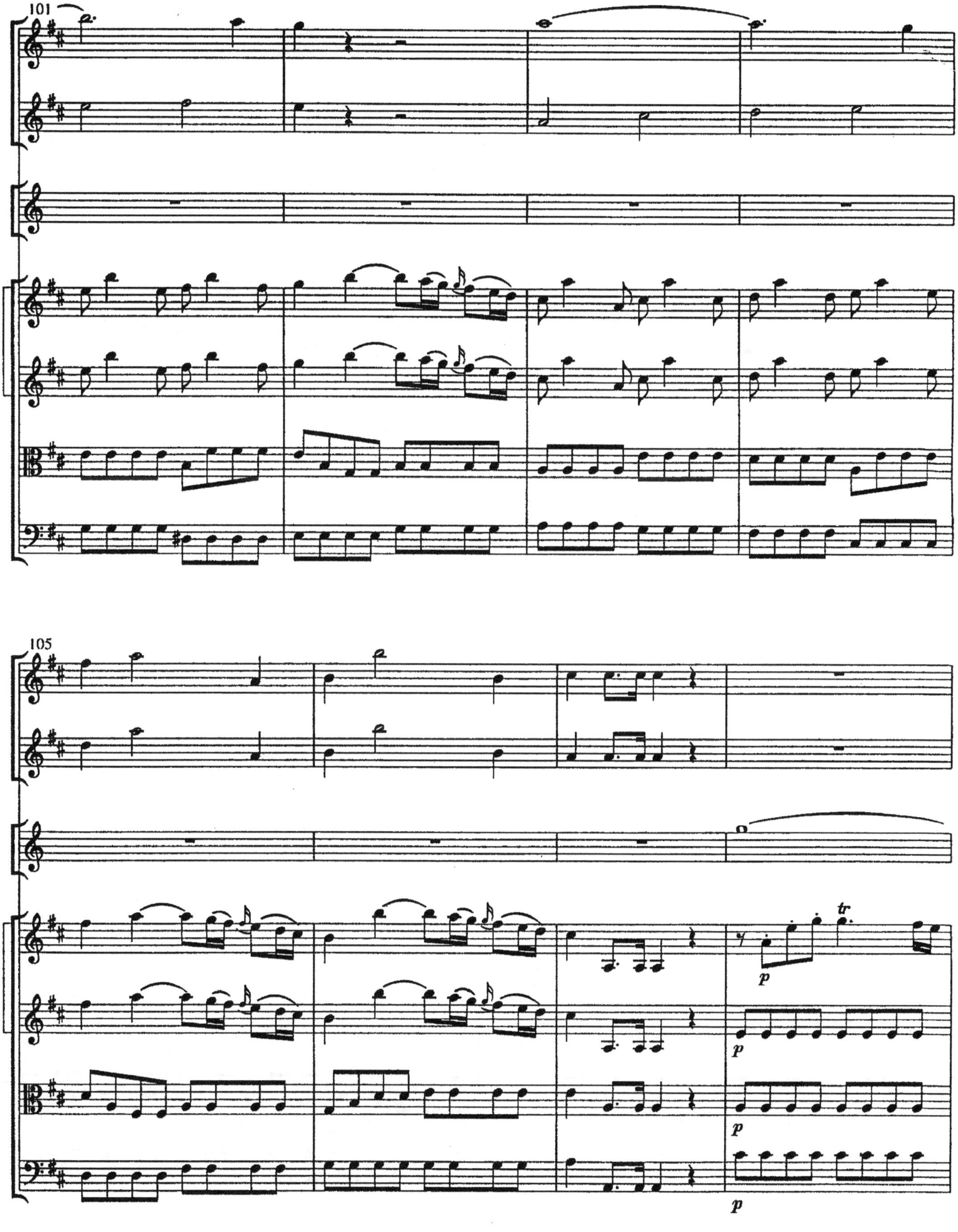
101
105
tr
p
p
p
p

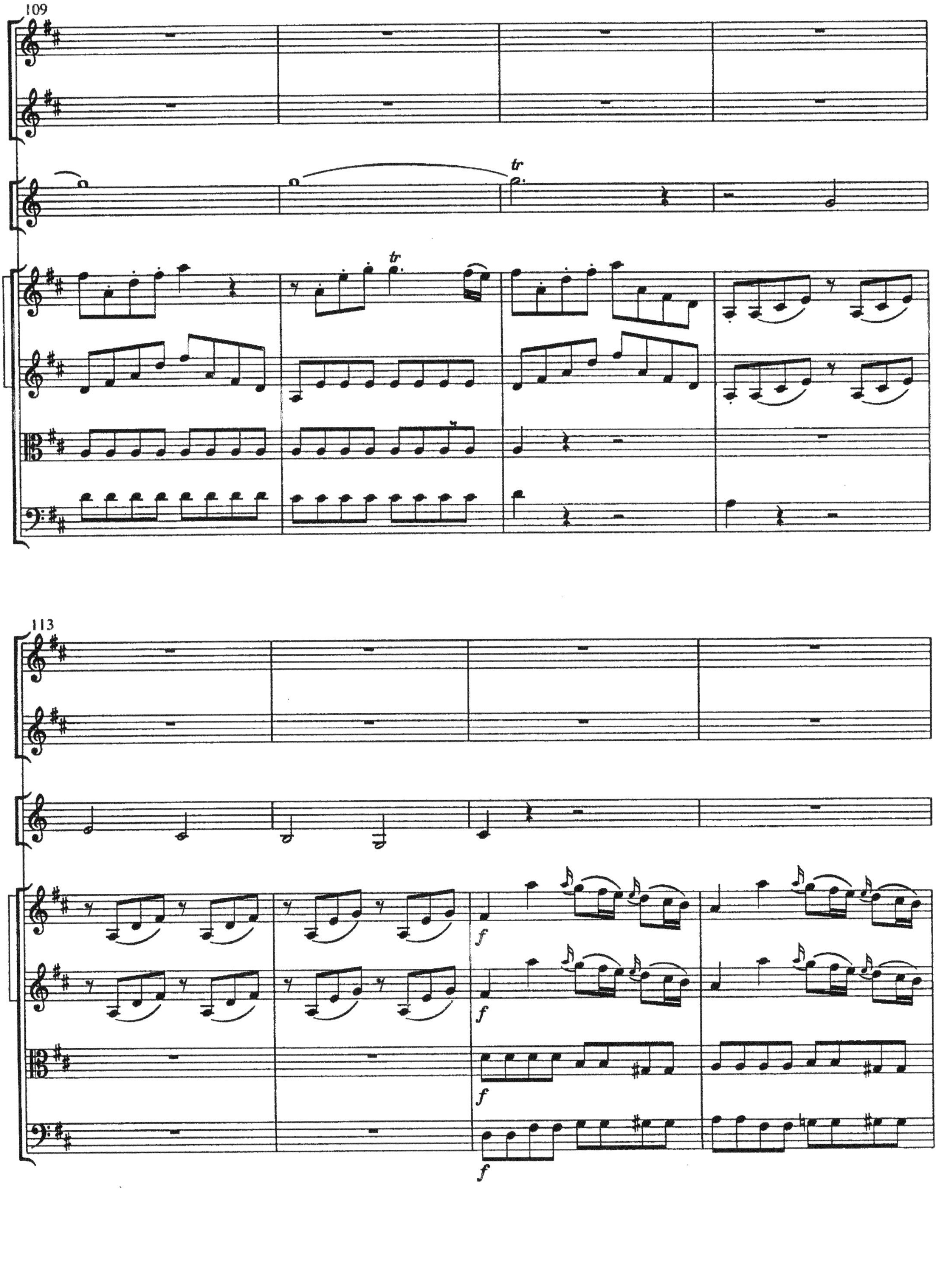
109
tr
113
f

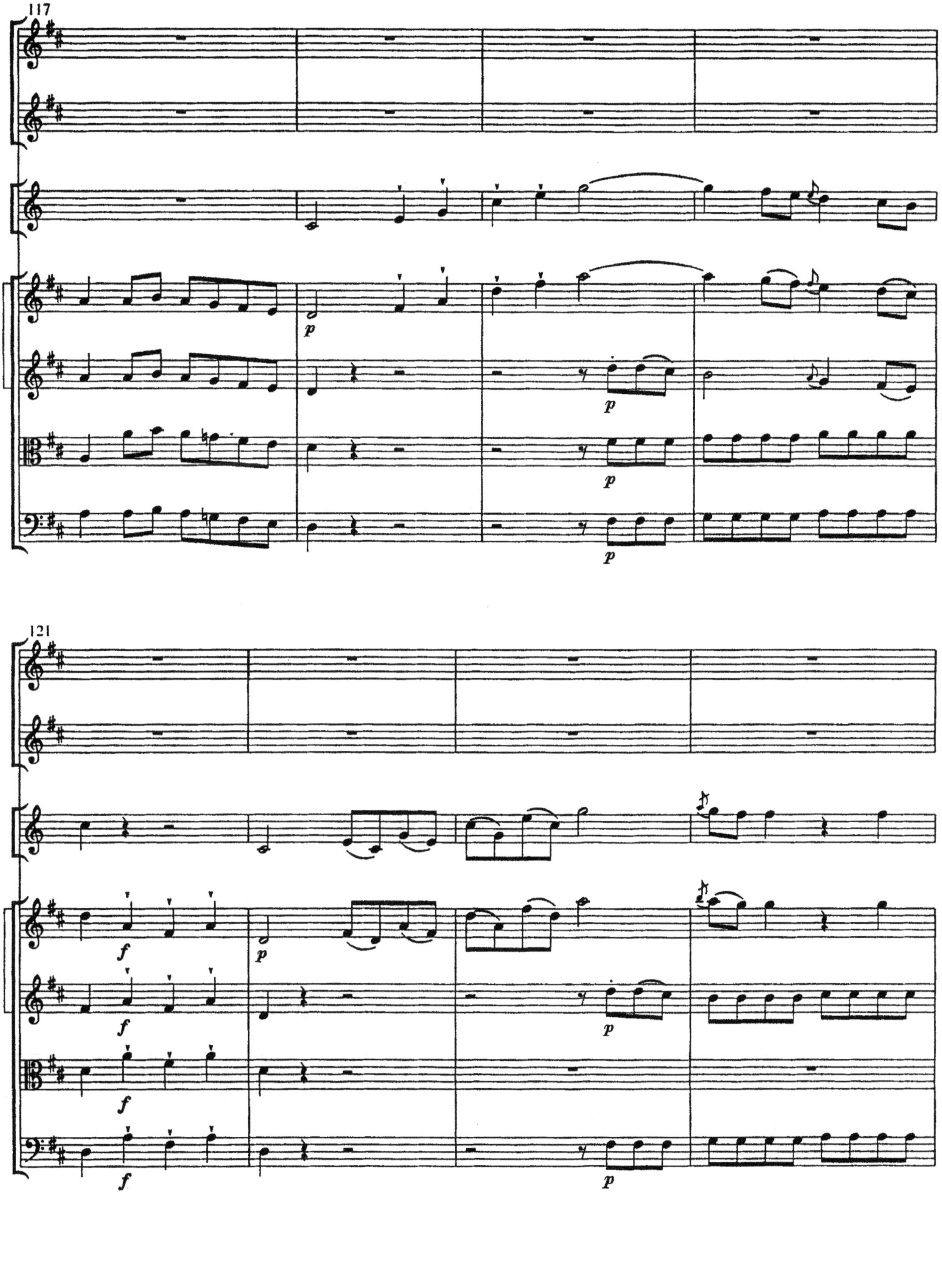
117
121

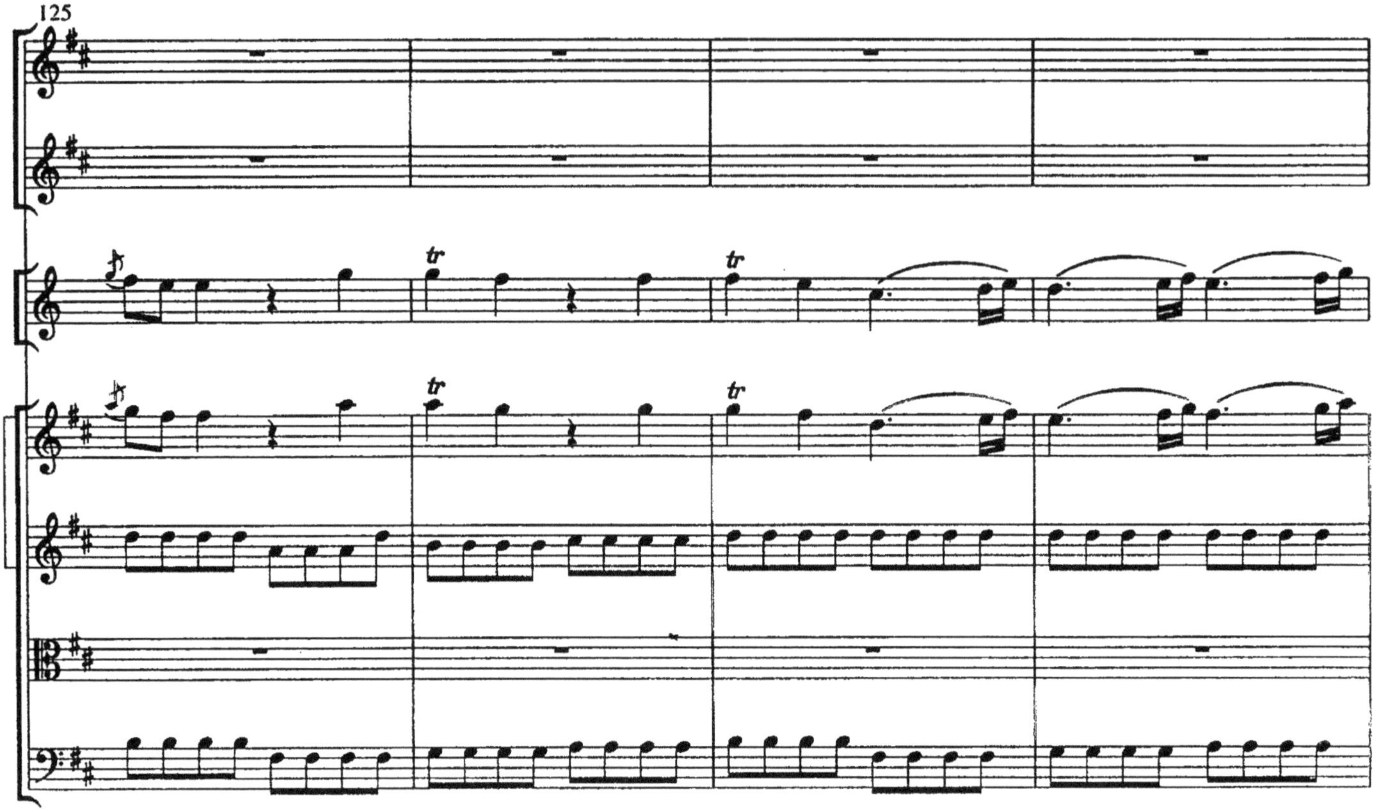
125
tr
tr
tr
tr

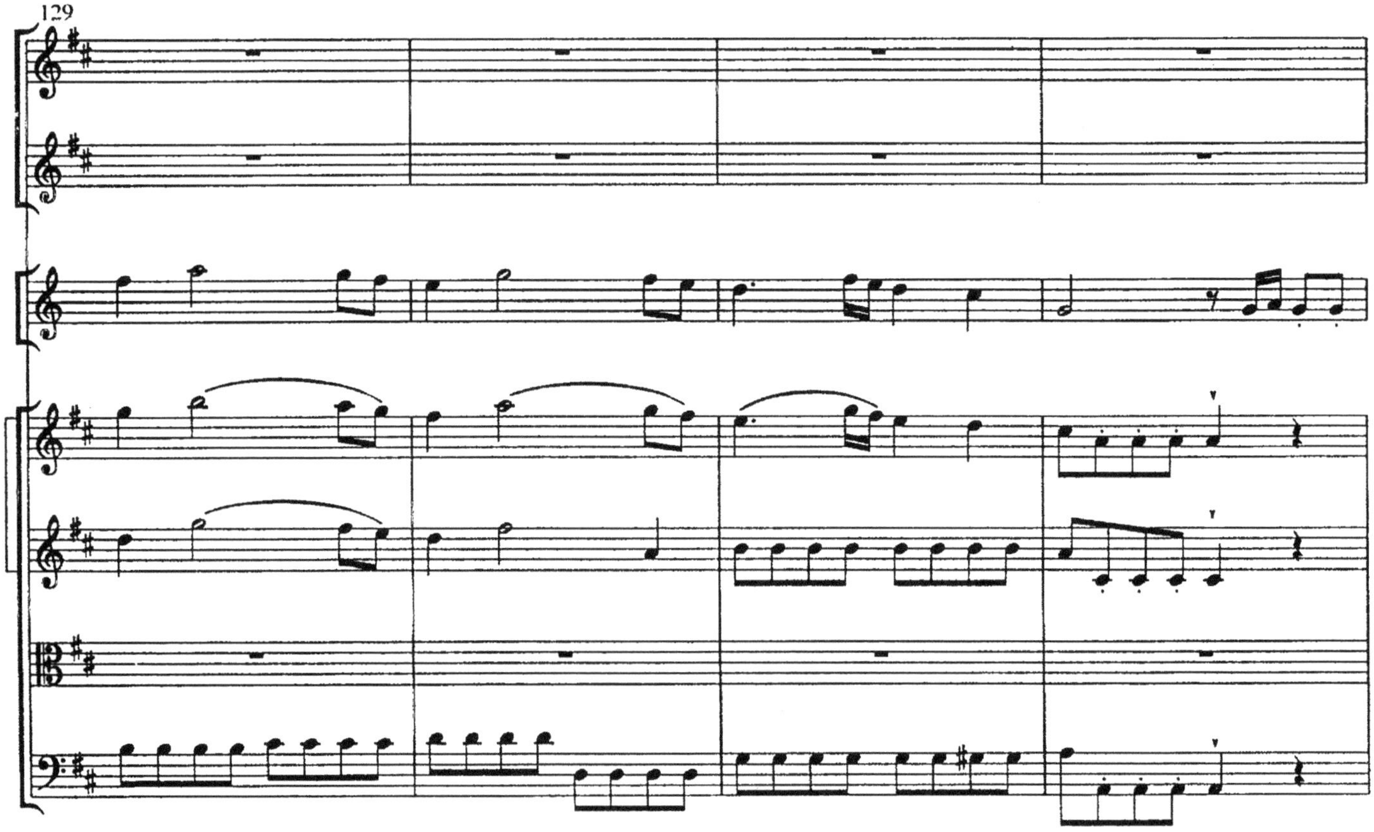
129

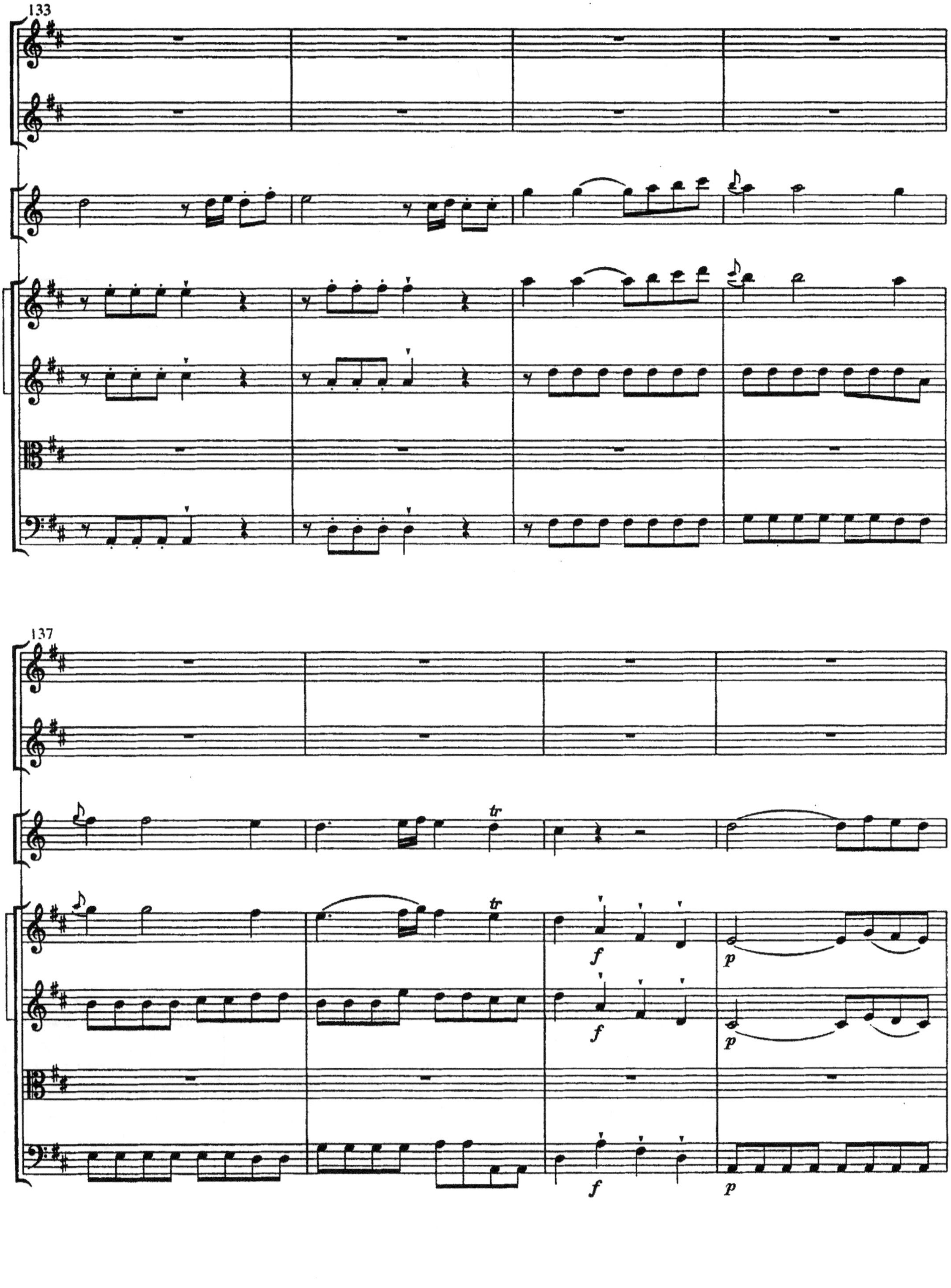
133
137
tr
f
p

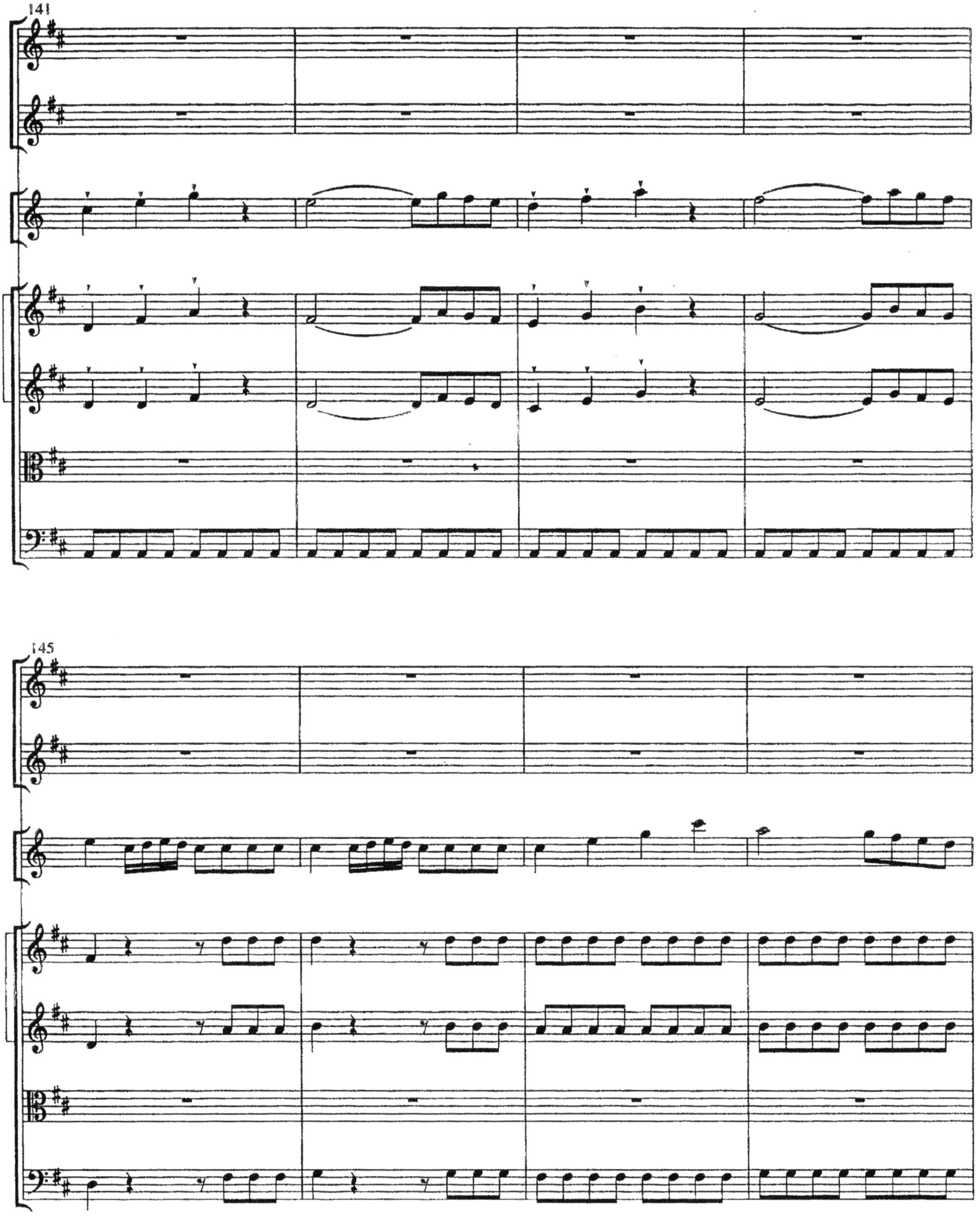
141
145

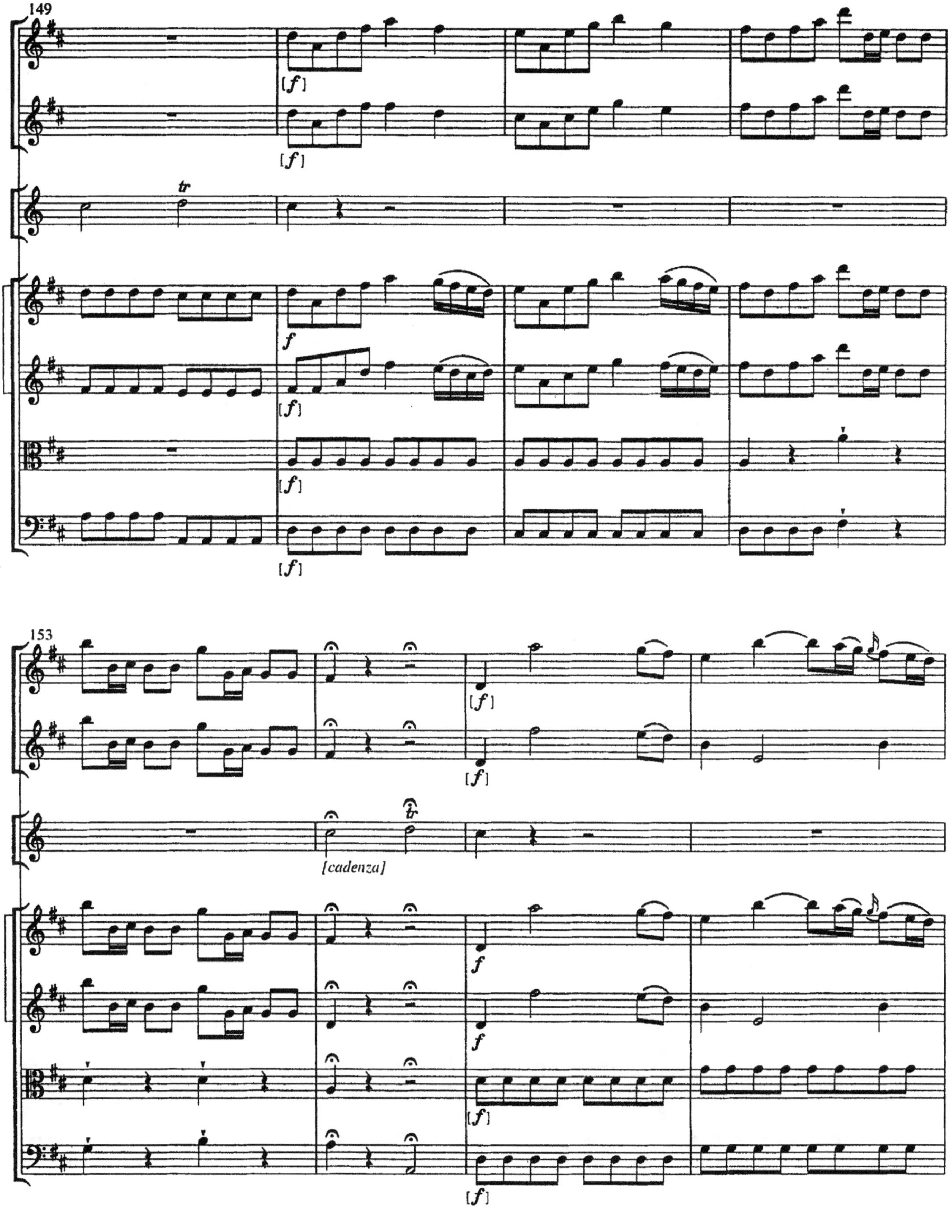
149
[f]
[f]
tr
f
[f]
[f]
[f]
153
[f]
[f]
tr
[cadenza]
f
f
[f]
[f]

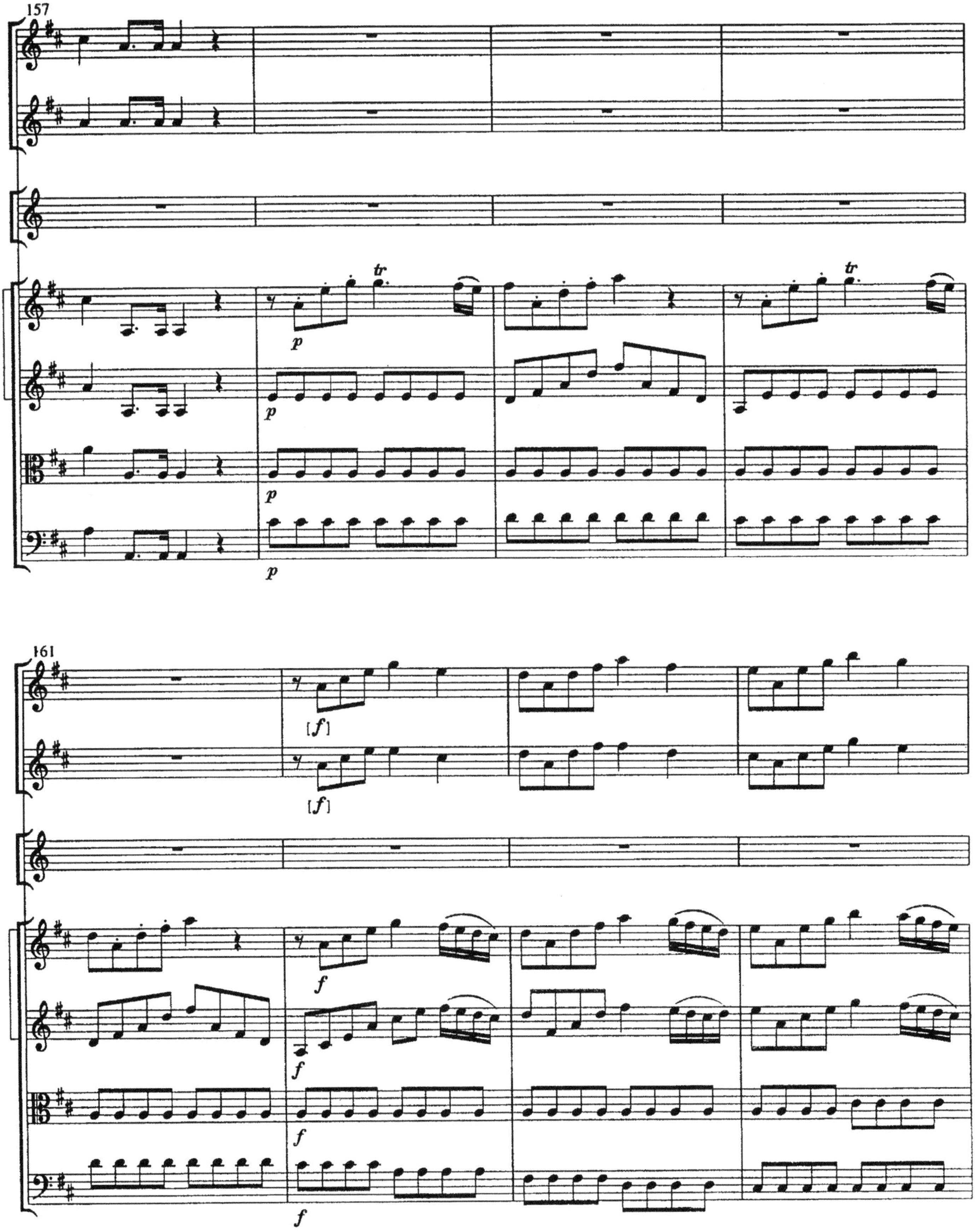
157
tr
p
p
p
p
tr
161
[f]
[f]
f
f
f
f

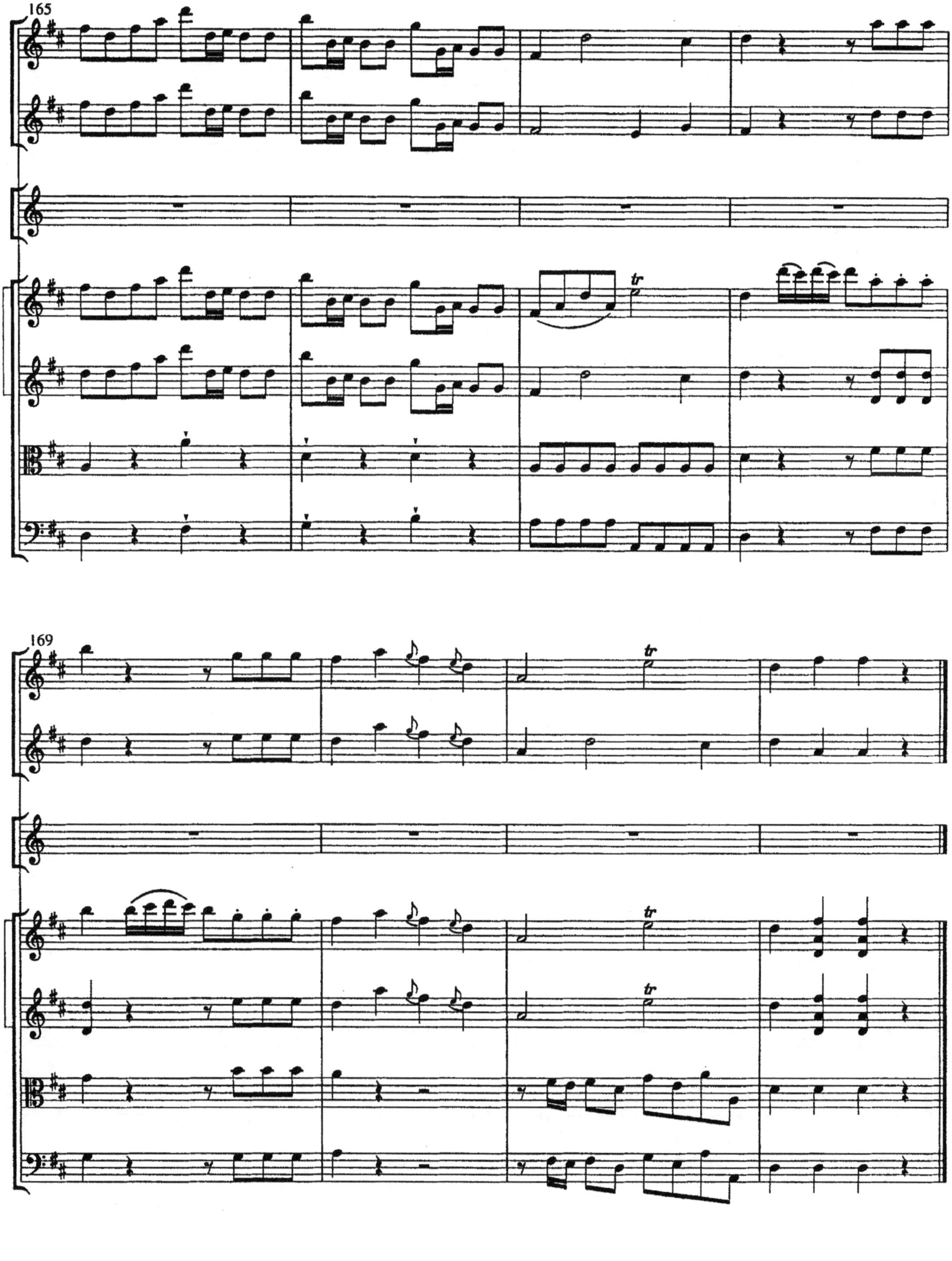
165
169

II

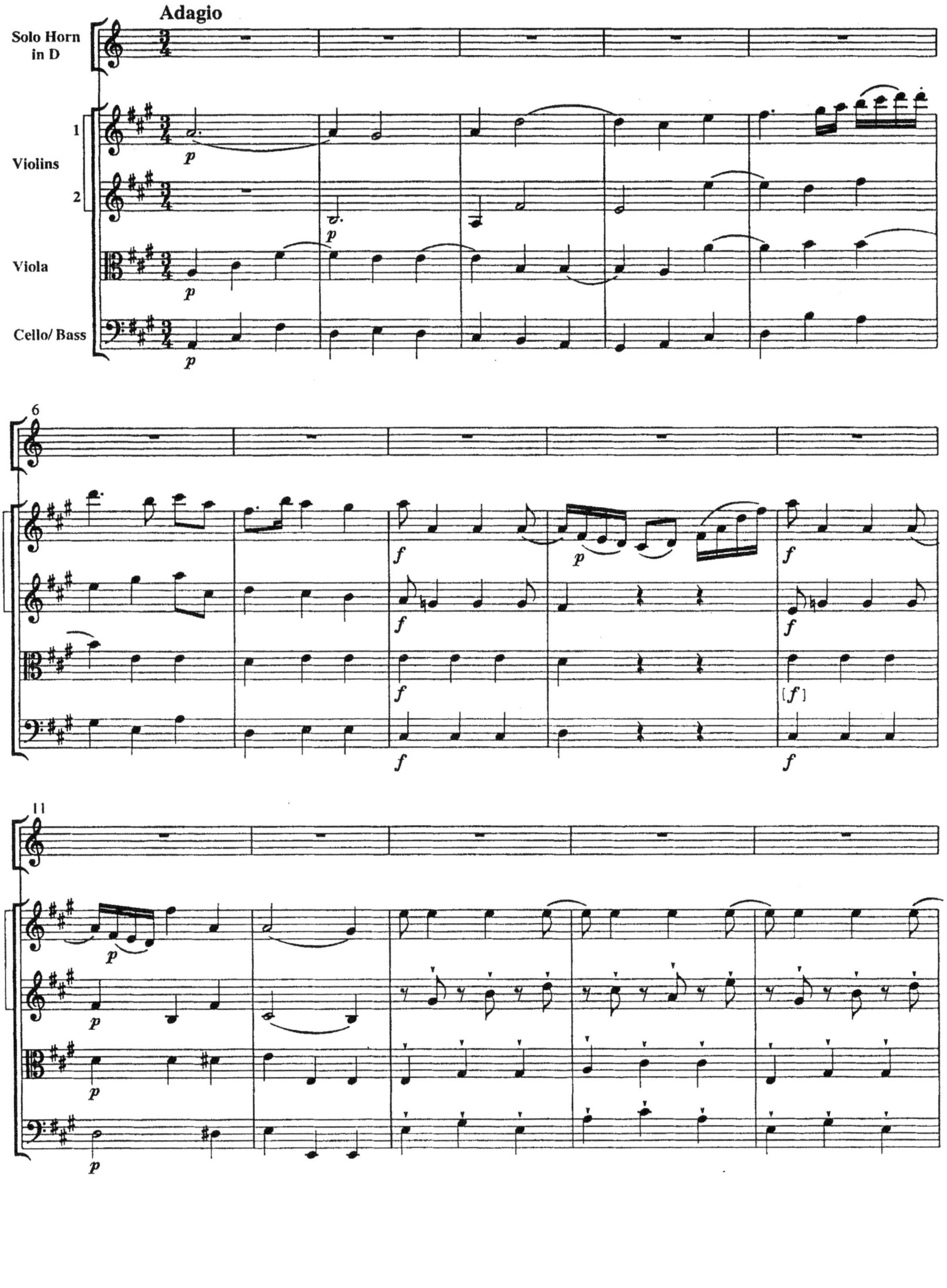

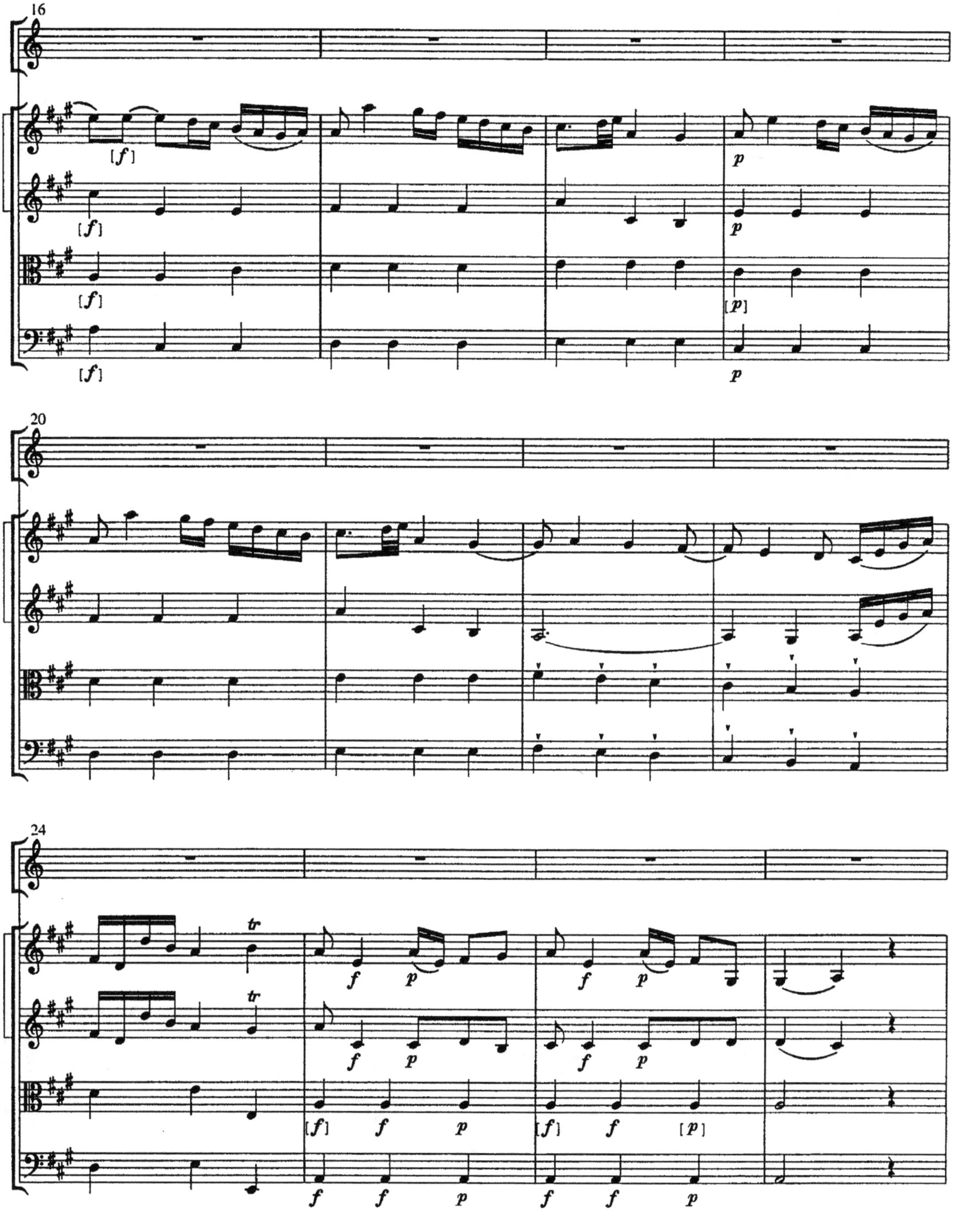
16
[f]
[f]
[f]
[f]
p
p
[p]
p
20
24
tr
tr
f p
f p
f p
f p
[f] f p
[f] f [p]
f f p
f f p

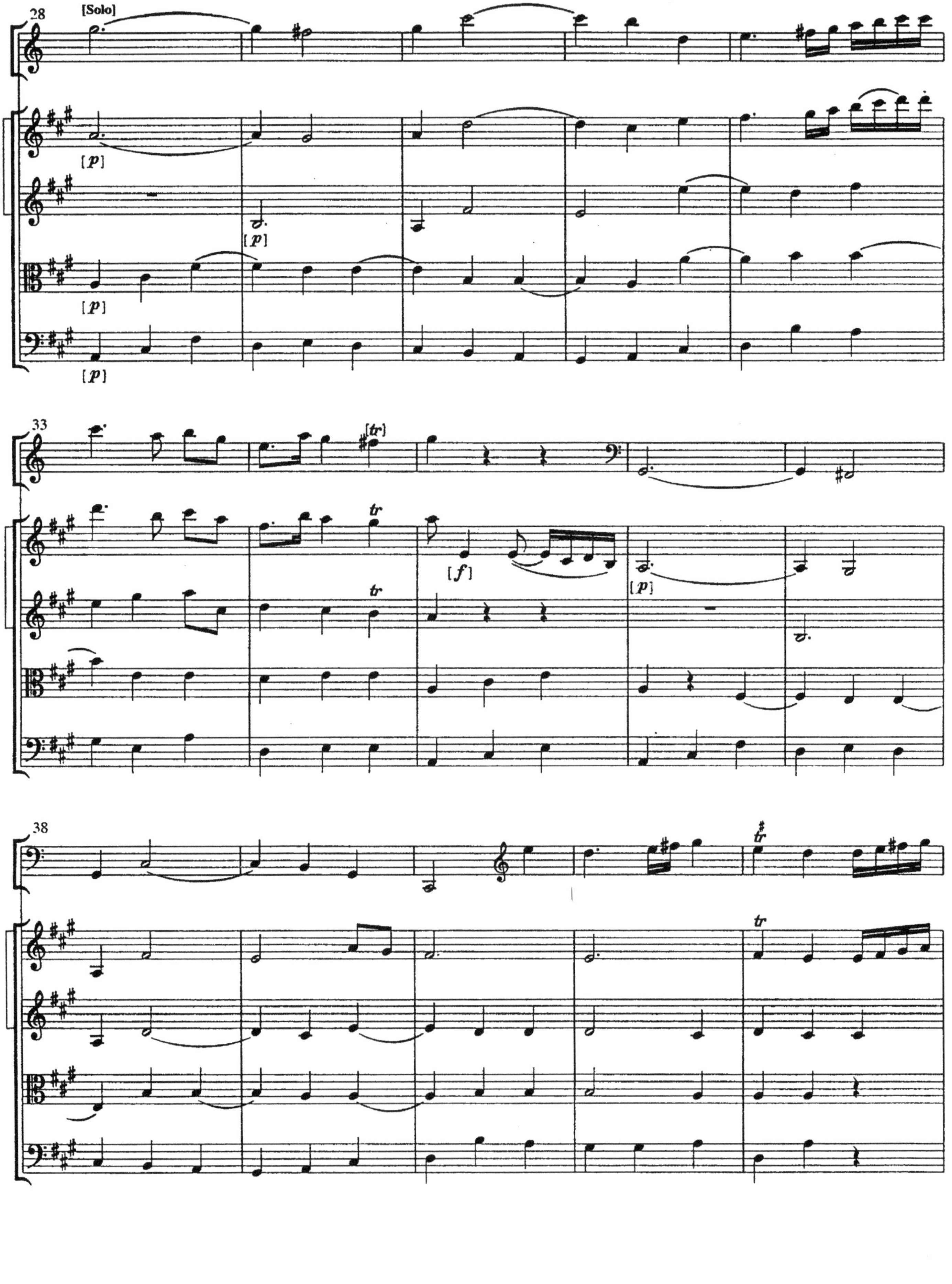
28
[Solo]
[p]
[p]
[p]
[p]
33
[tr]
tr
tr
[f]
[p]
38
tr
tr

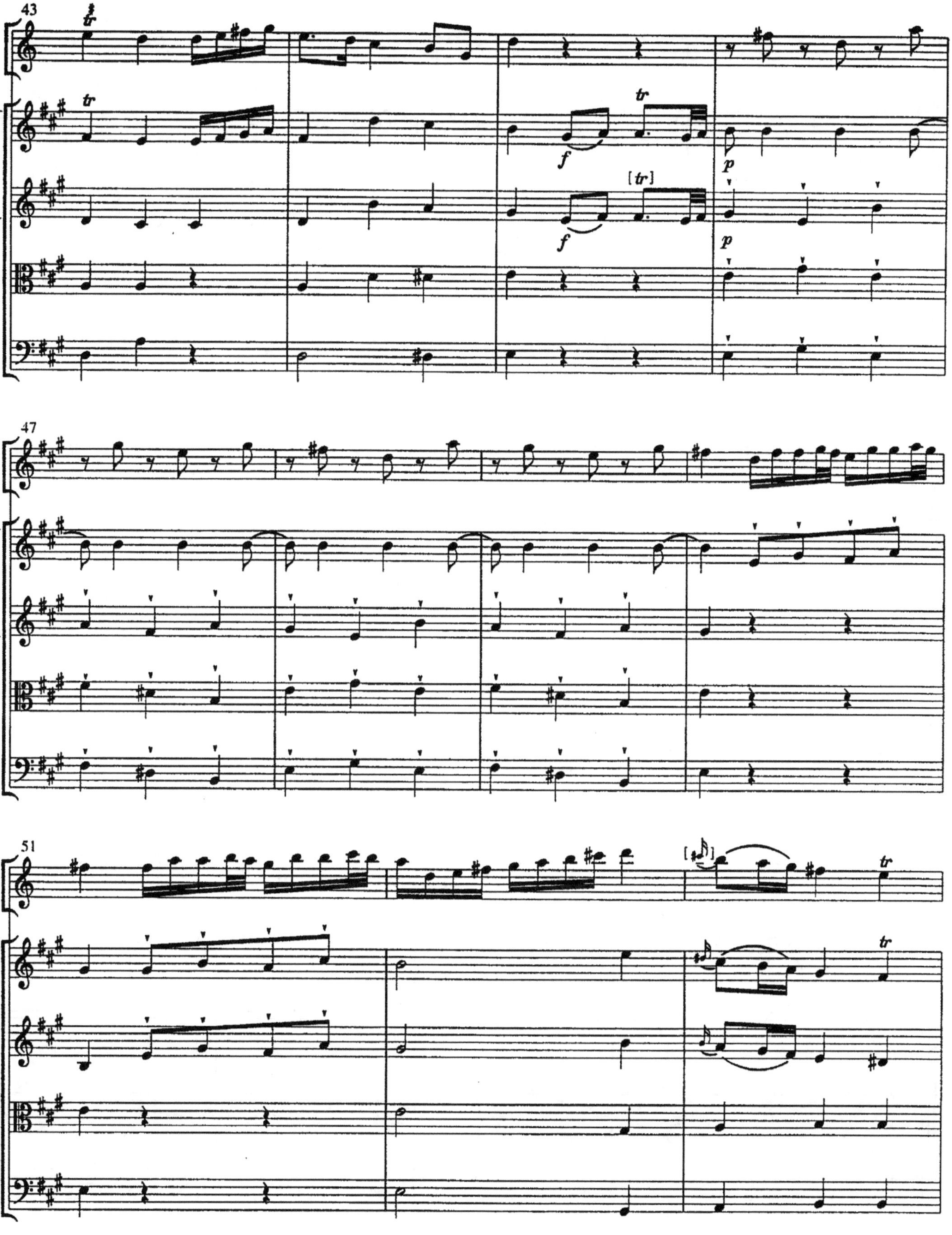
43
tr
f
[tr]
p
47
51
tr

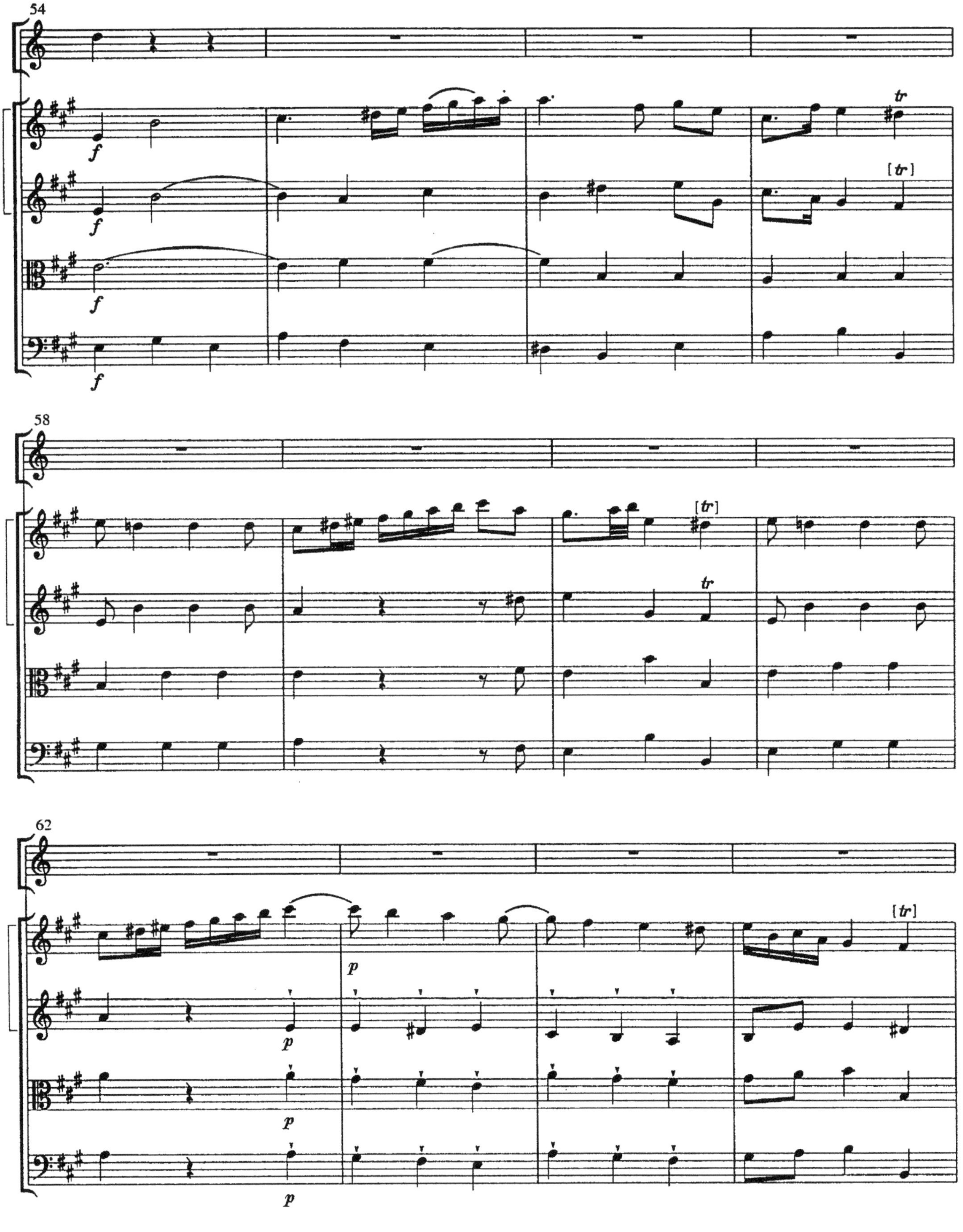
54
58
62
tr
[tr]
f
p

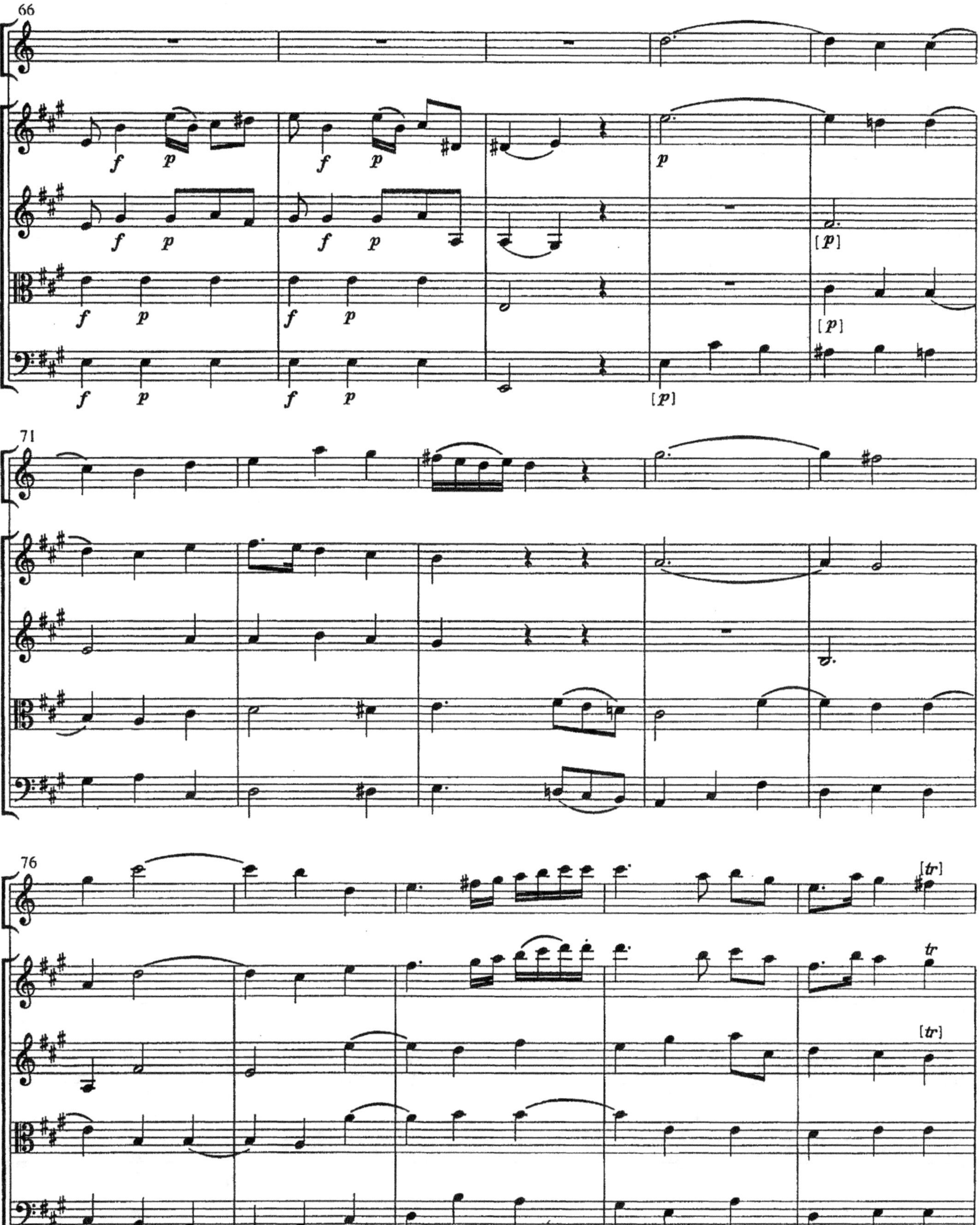
66
f
p
[p]
71
76
tr
[tr]

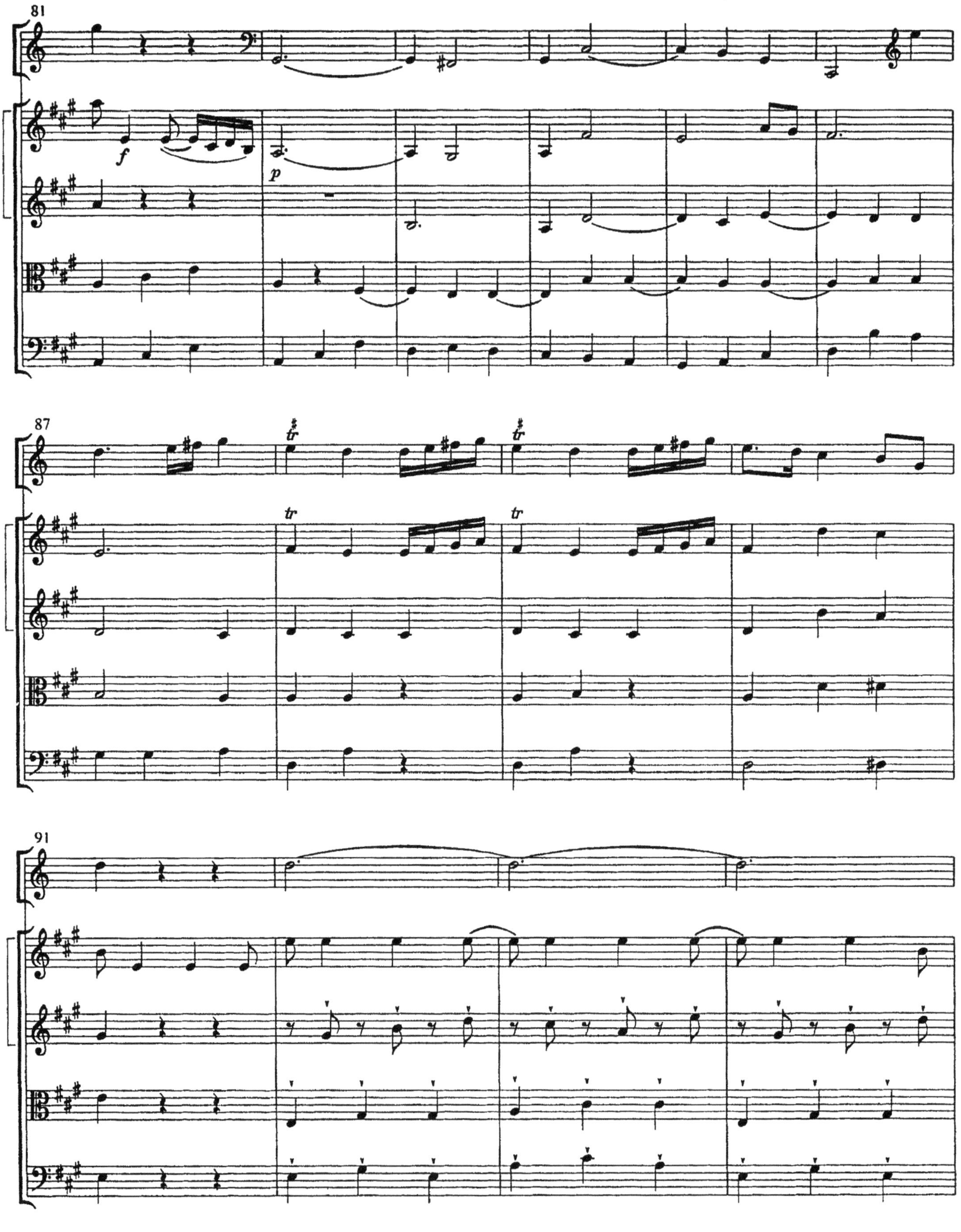
81
f
p
87
tr
tr
tr
tr
91

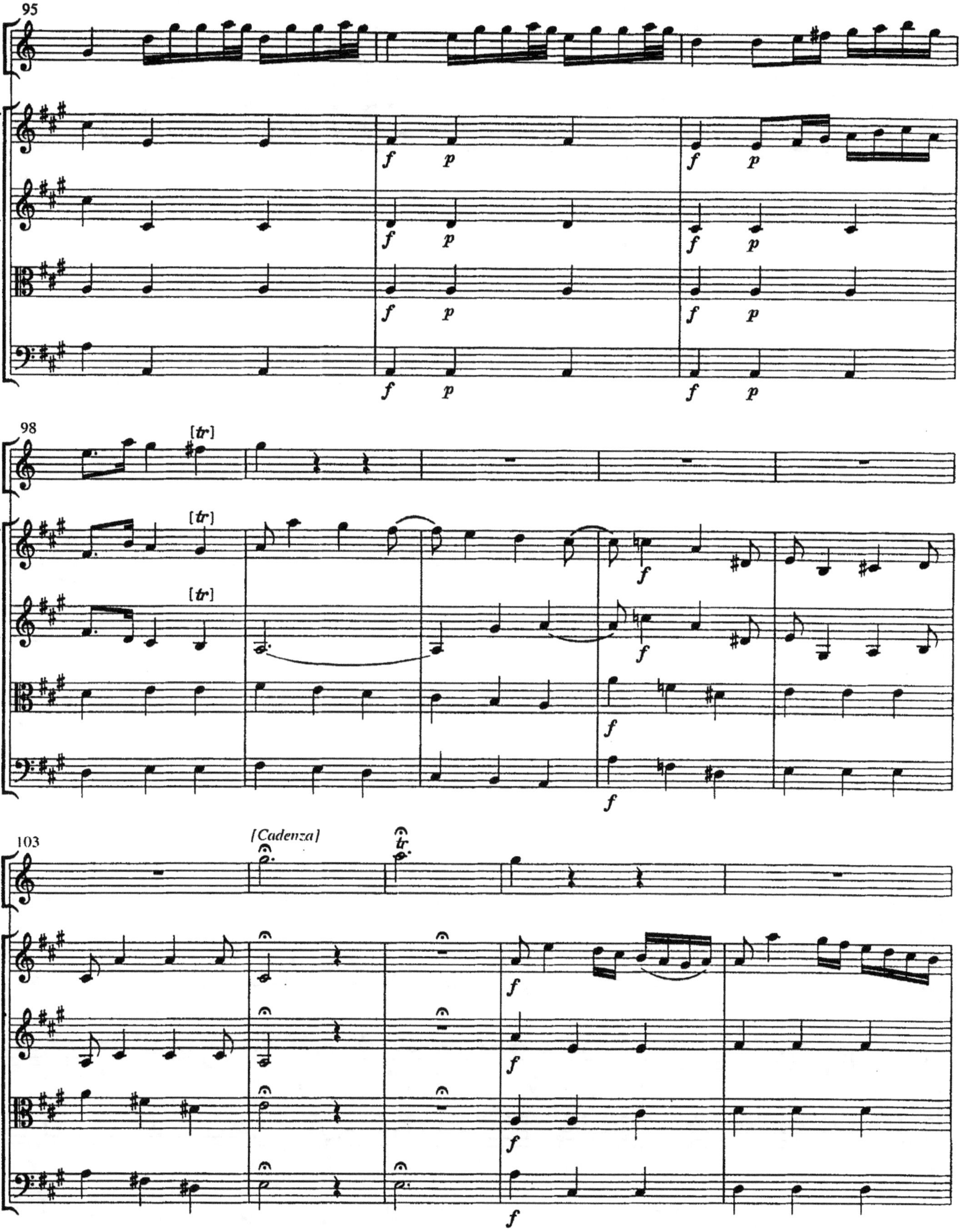
95
98
[tr]
103
[Cadenza]
tr
f
p

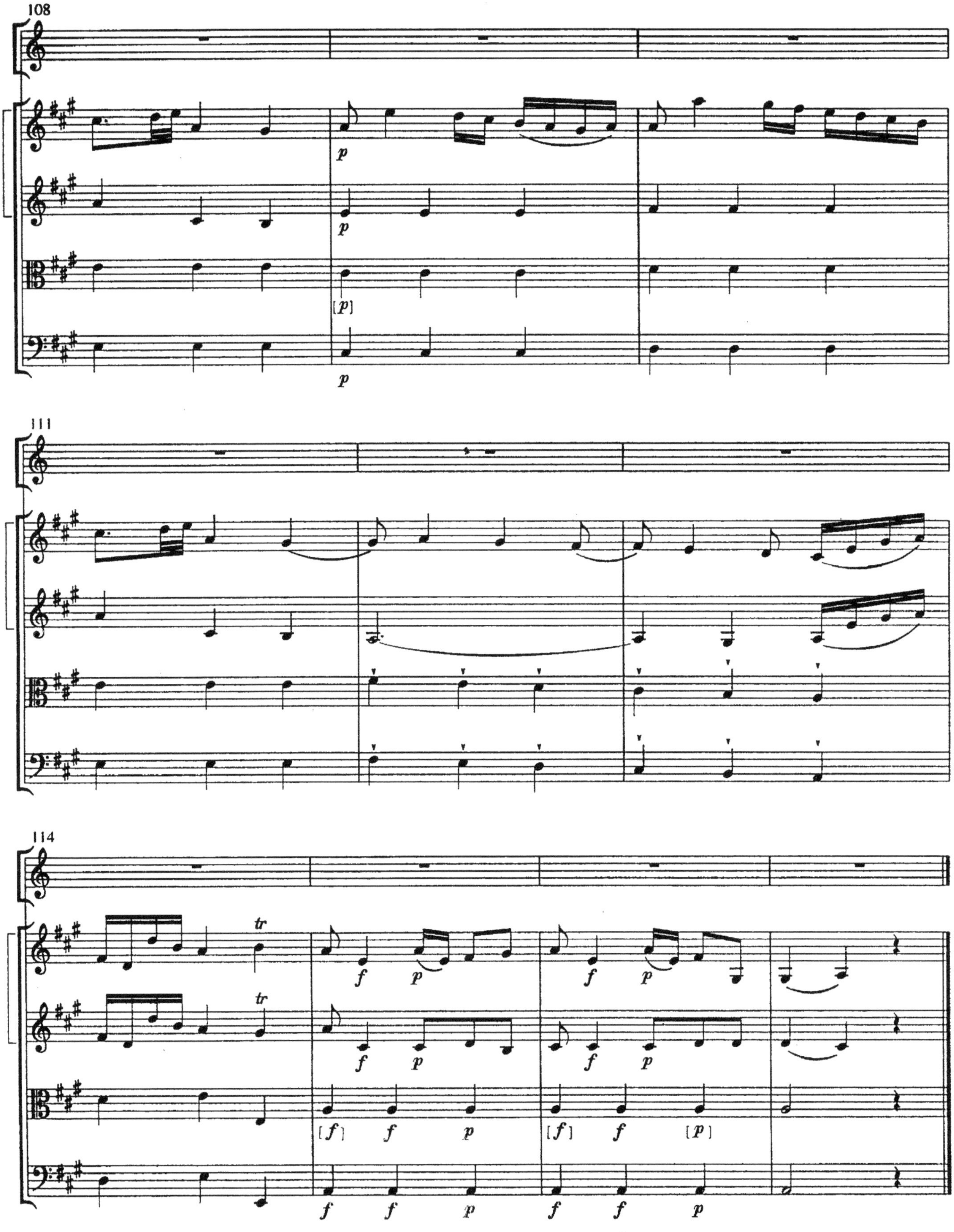
108
111
114

III

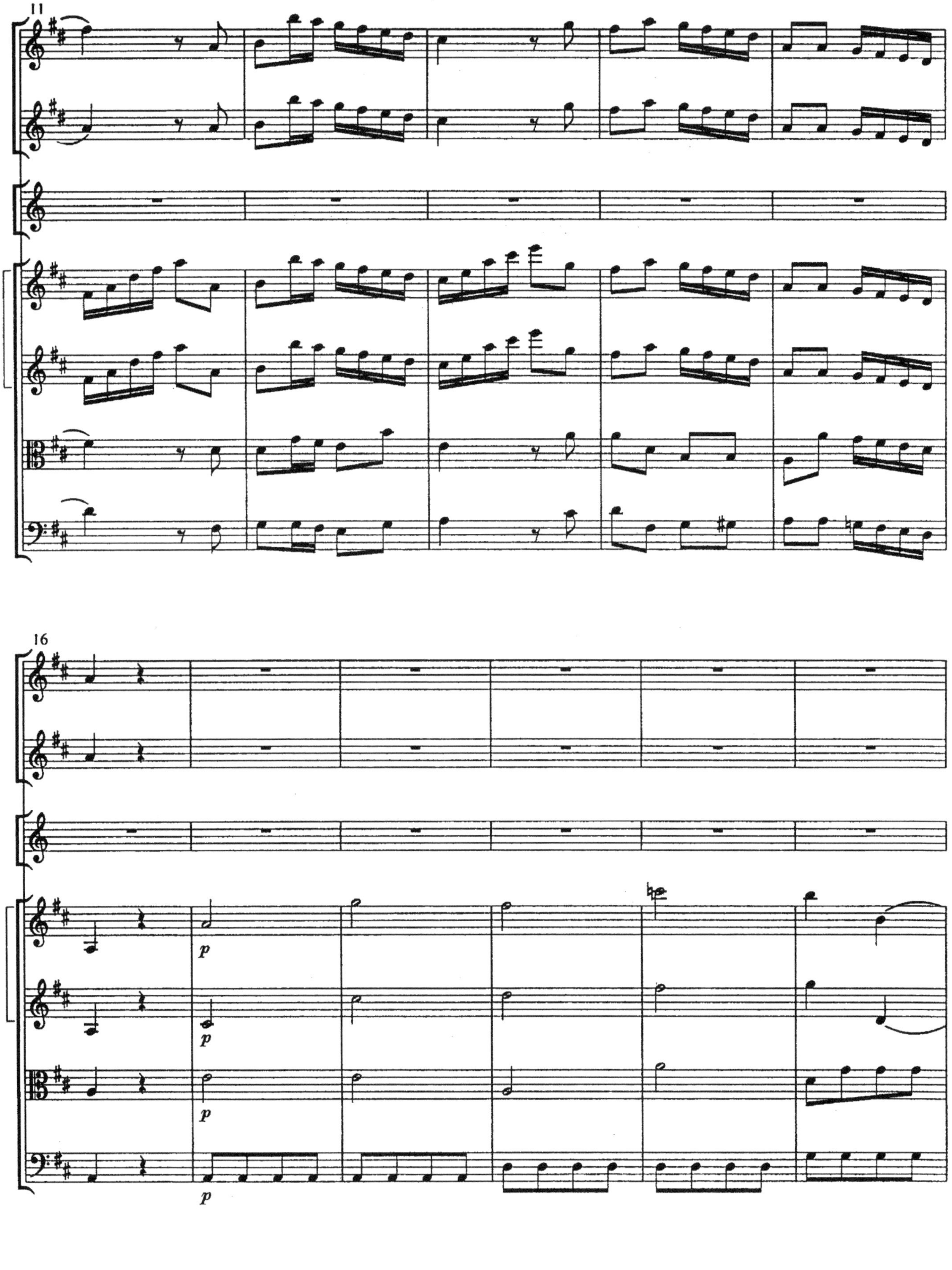
11
16
p
p
p
p

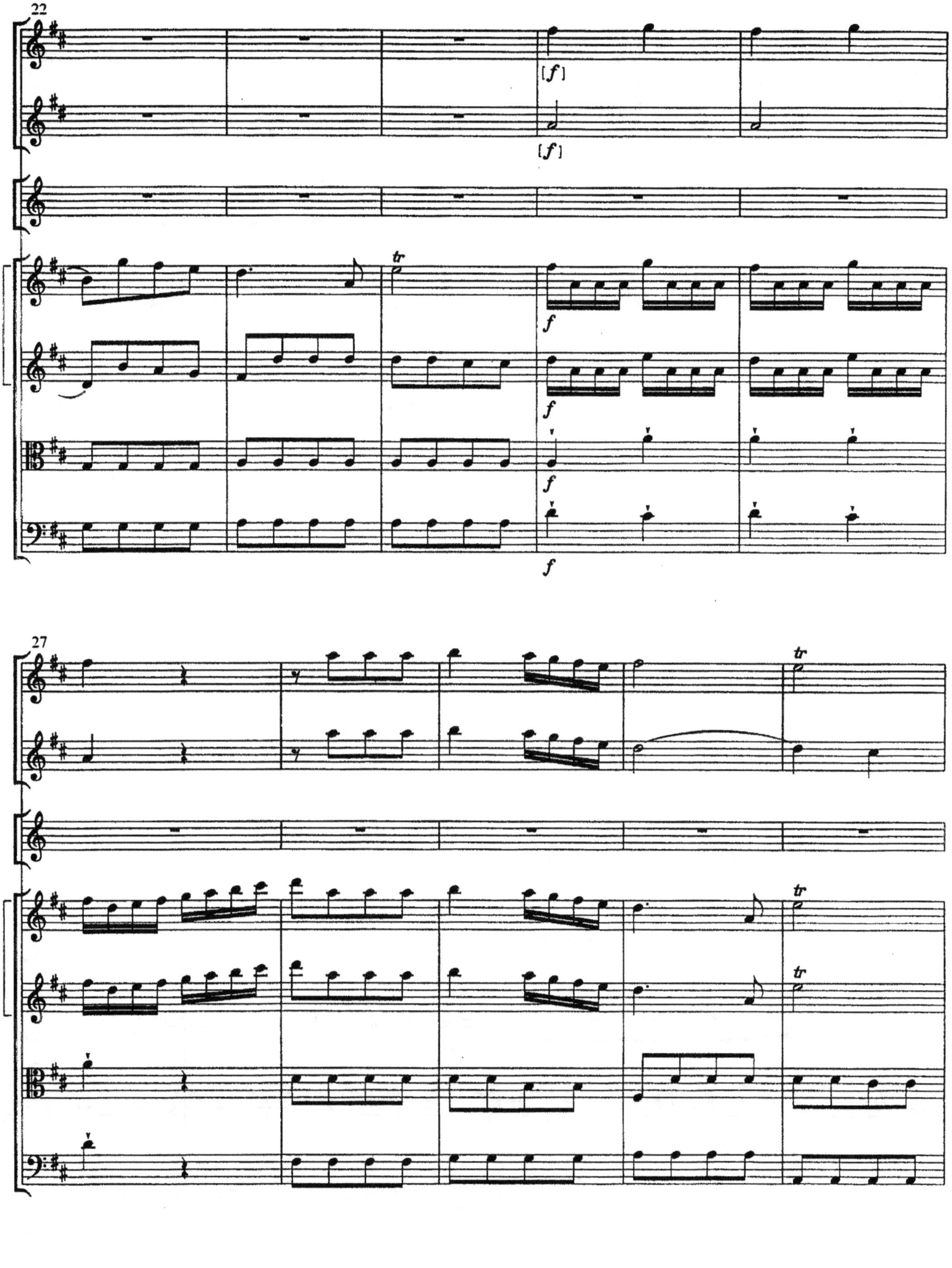
22
[f]
[f]
tr
f
f
f
f
27
tr
tr
tr

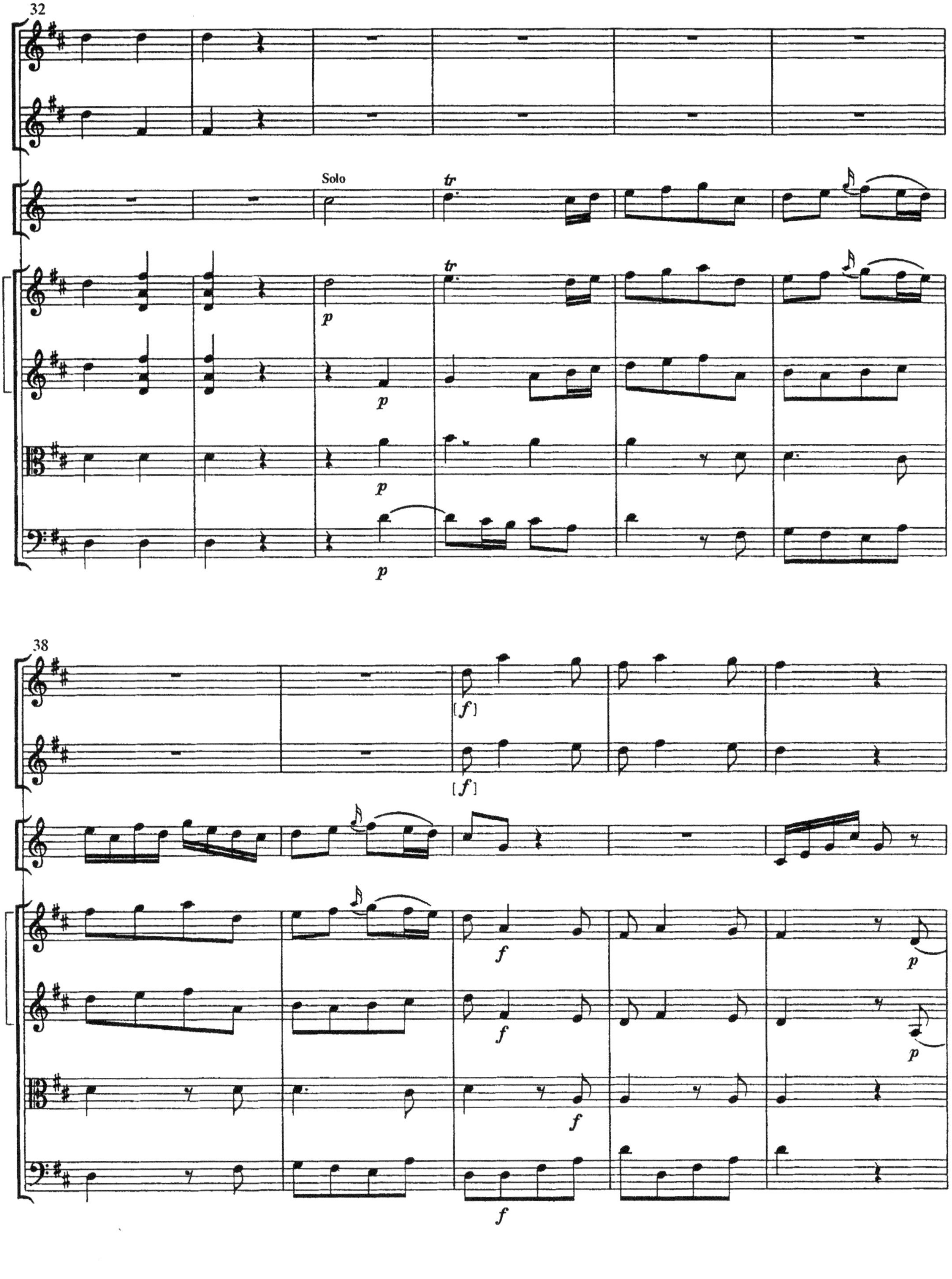
32
Solo
tr
tr
p
p
p
p
38
[f]
[f]
f
f
f
f
p
p

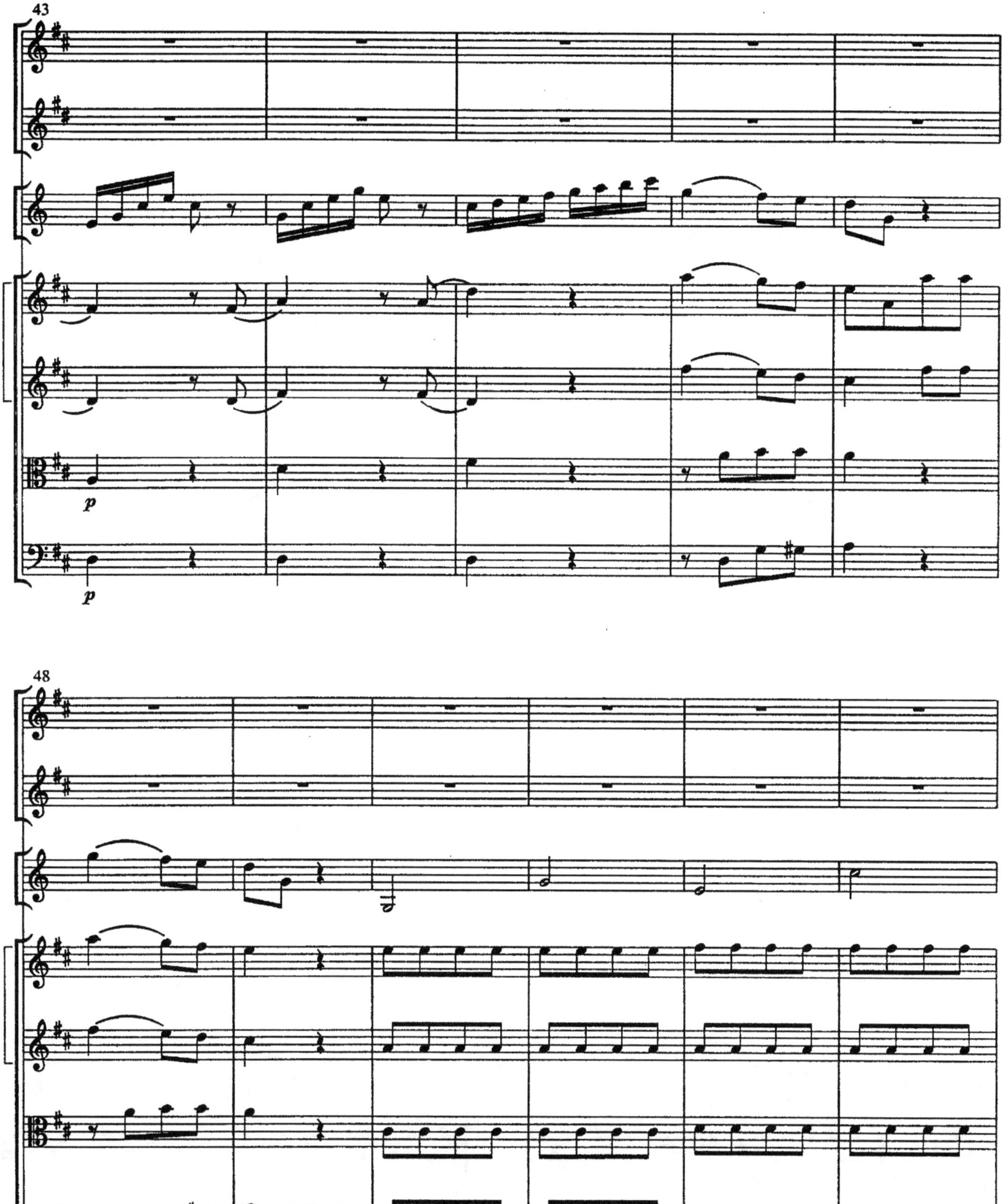
43
p
p
48

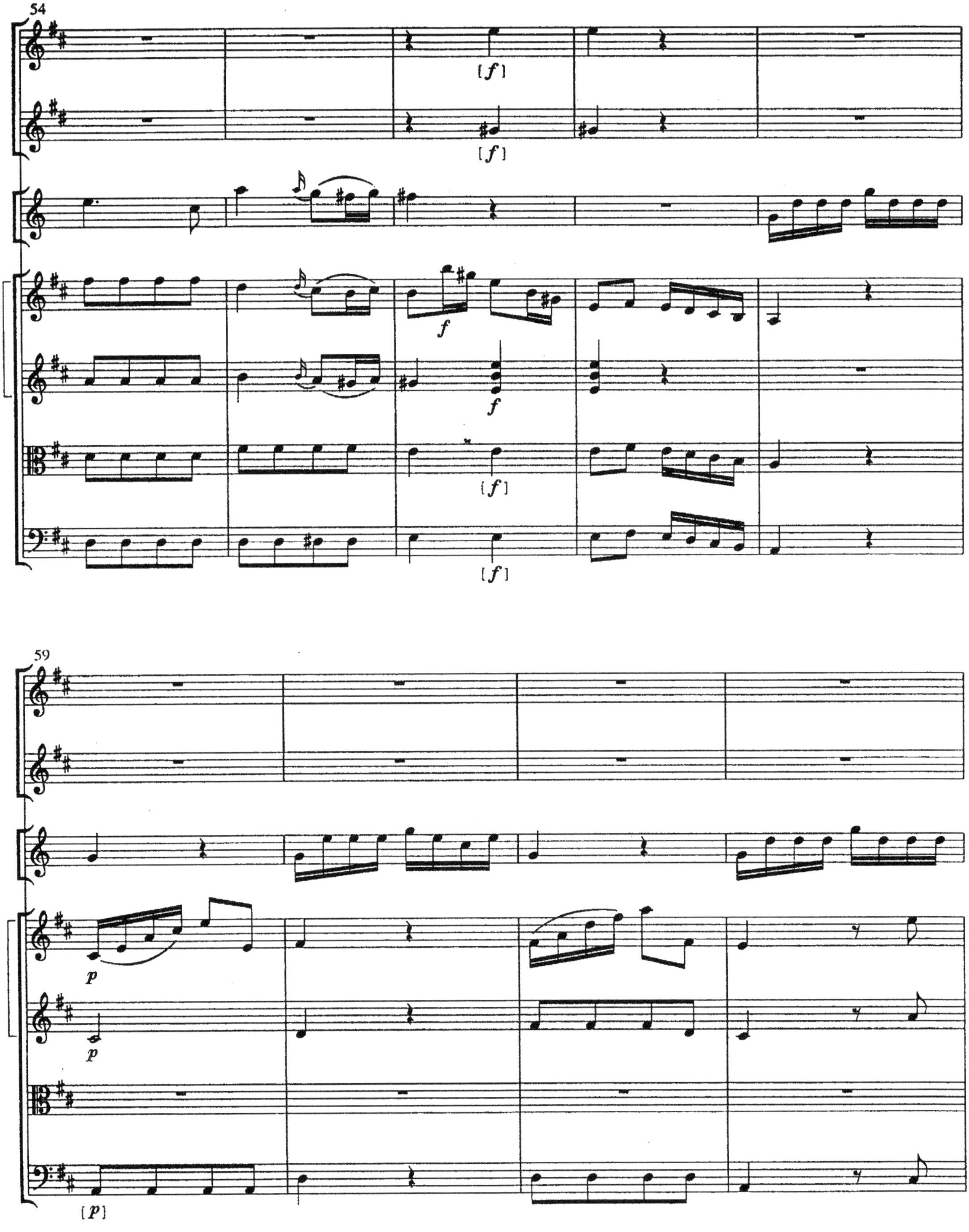
54
59

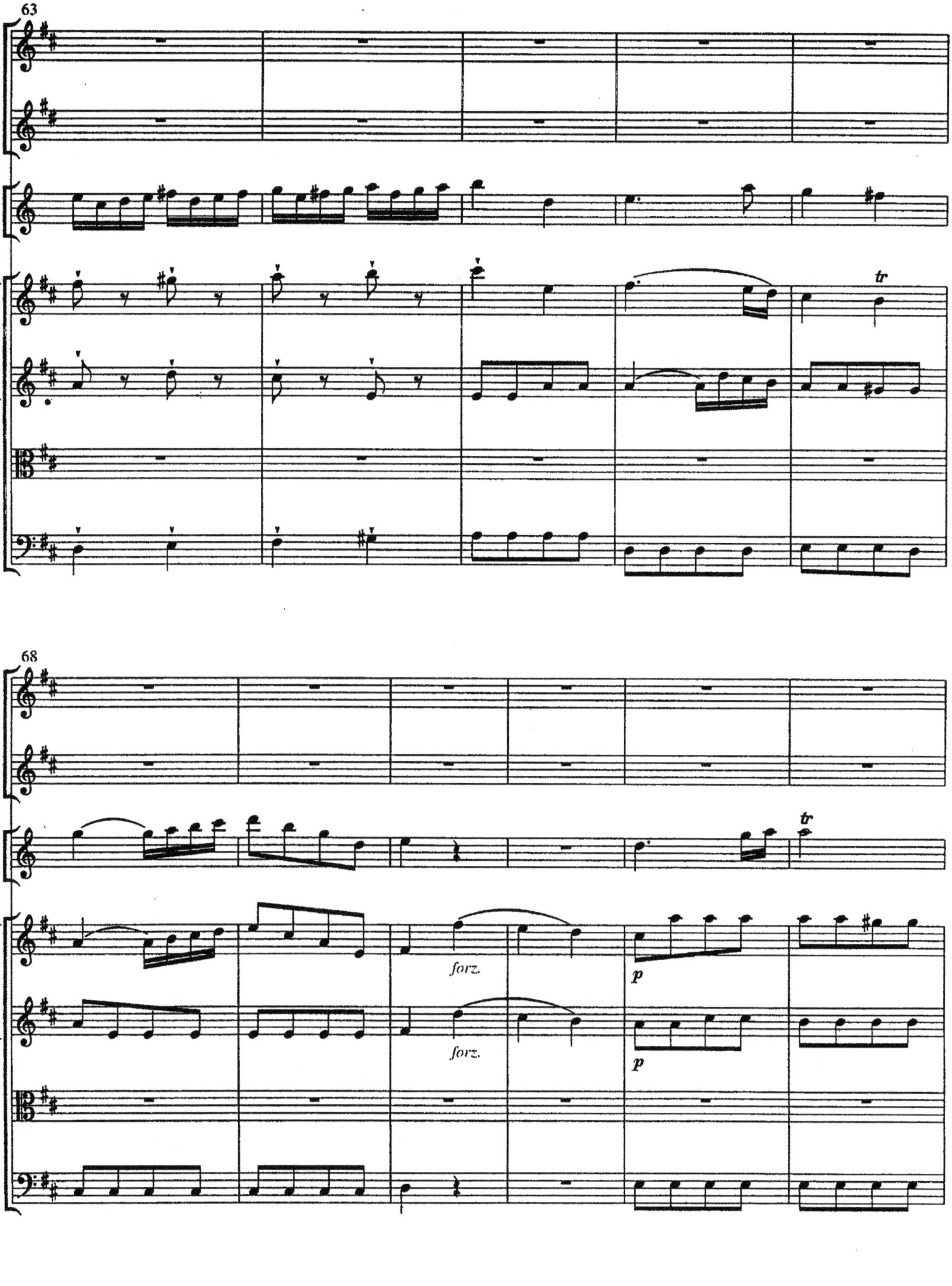
63
tr
68
tr
forz.
forz.
p
p

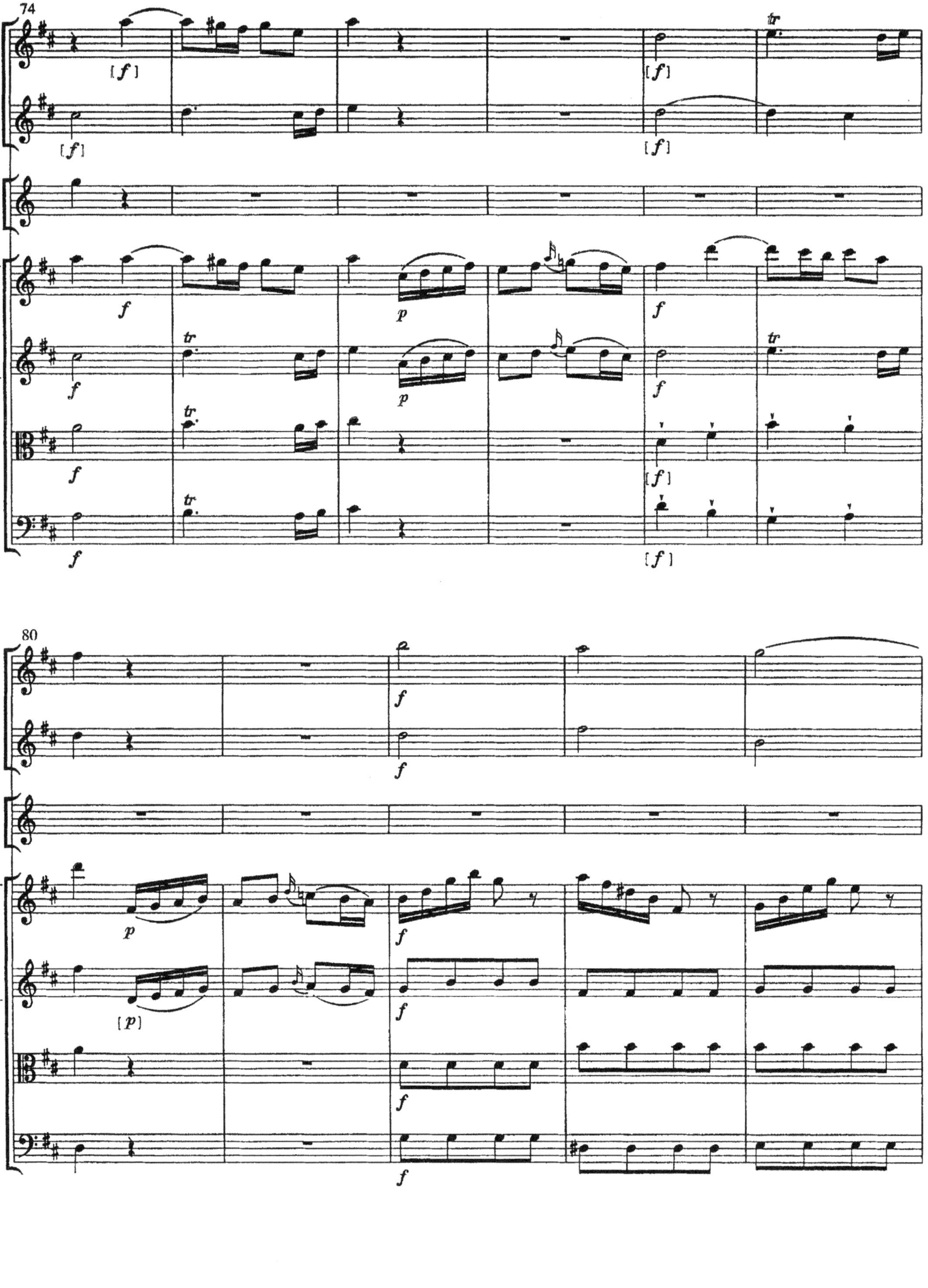
74
80

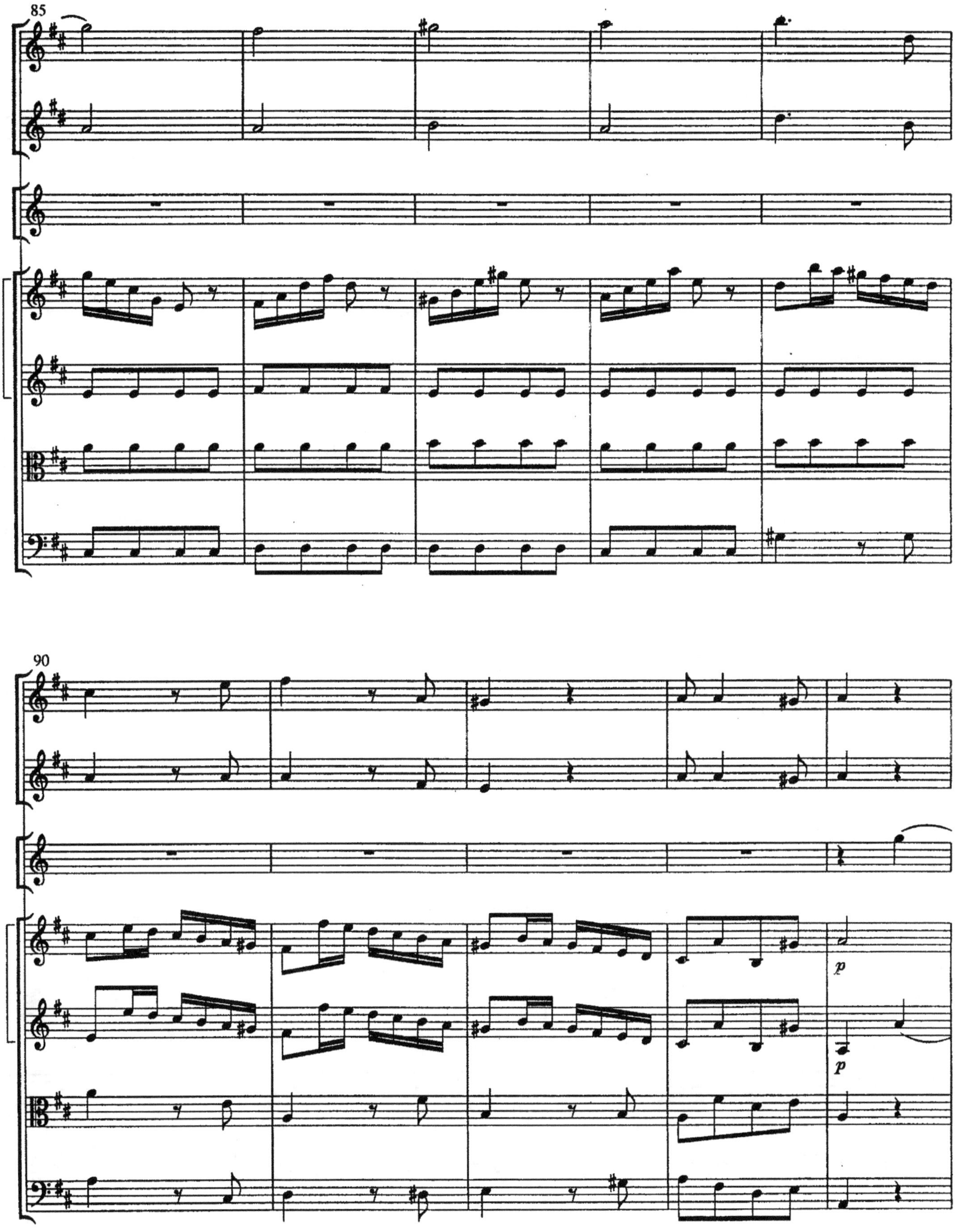
85
90
p
p

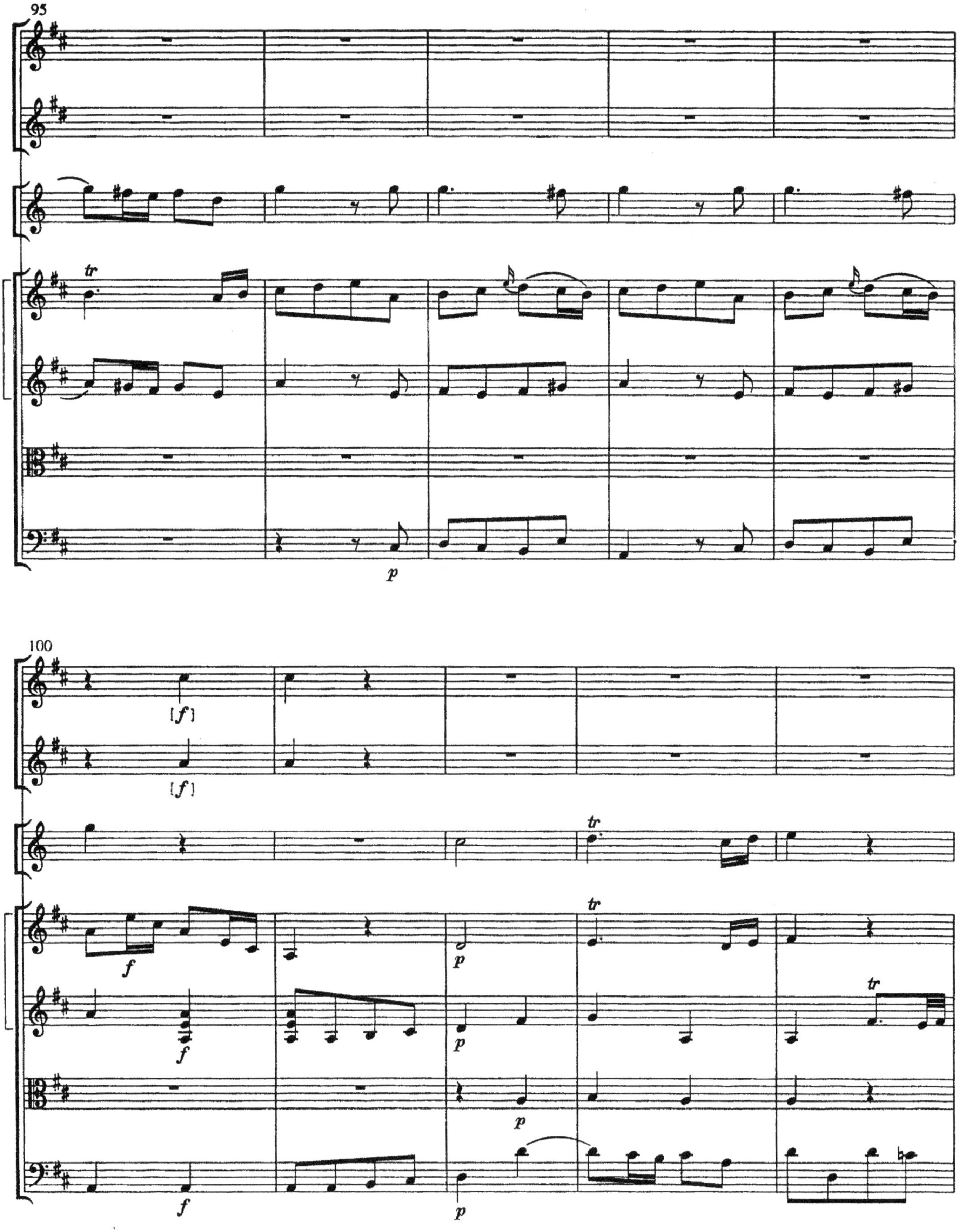
95
tr
p
100
[f]
[f]
f
tr
tr
p
tr

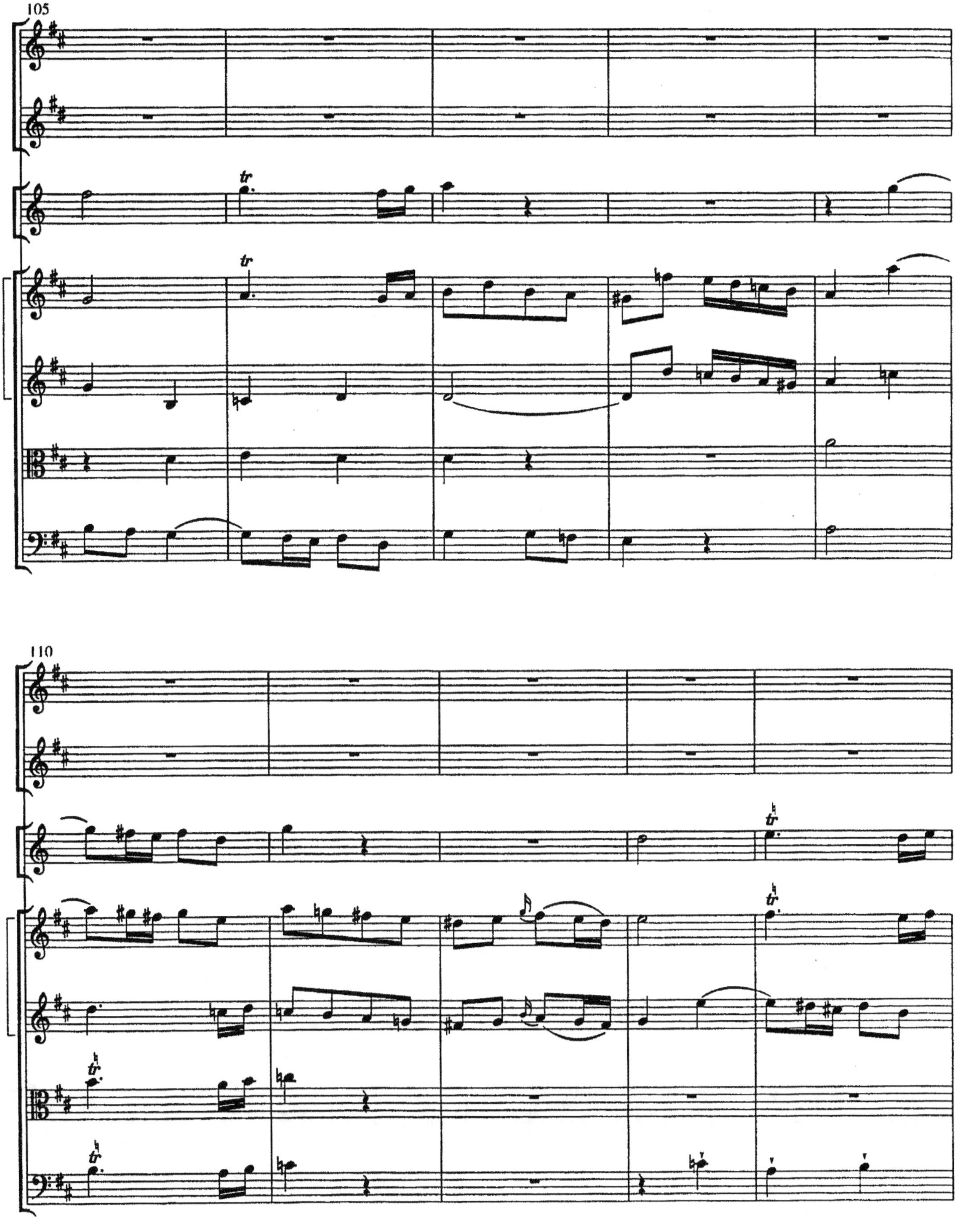
105
110

42

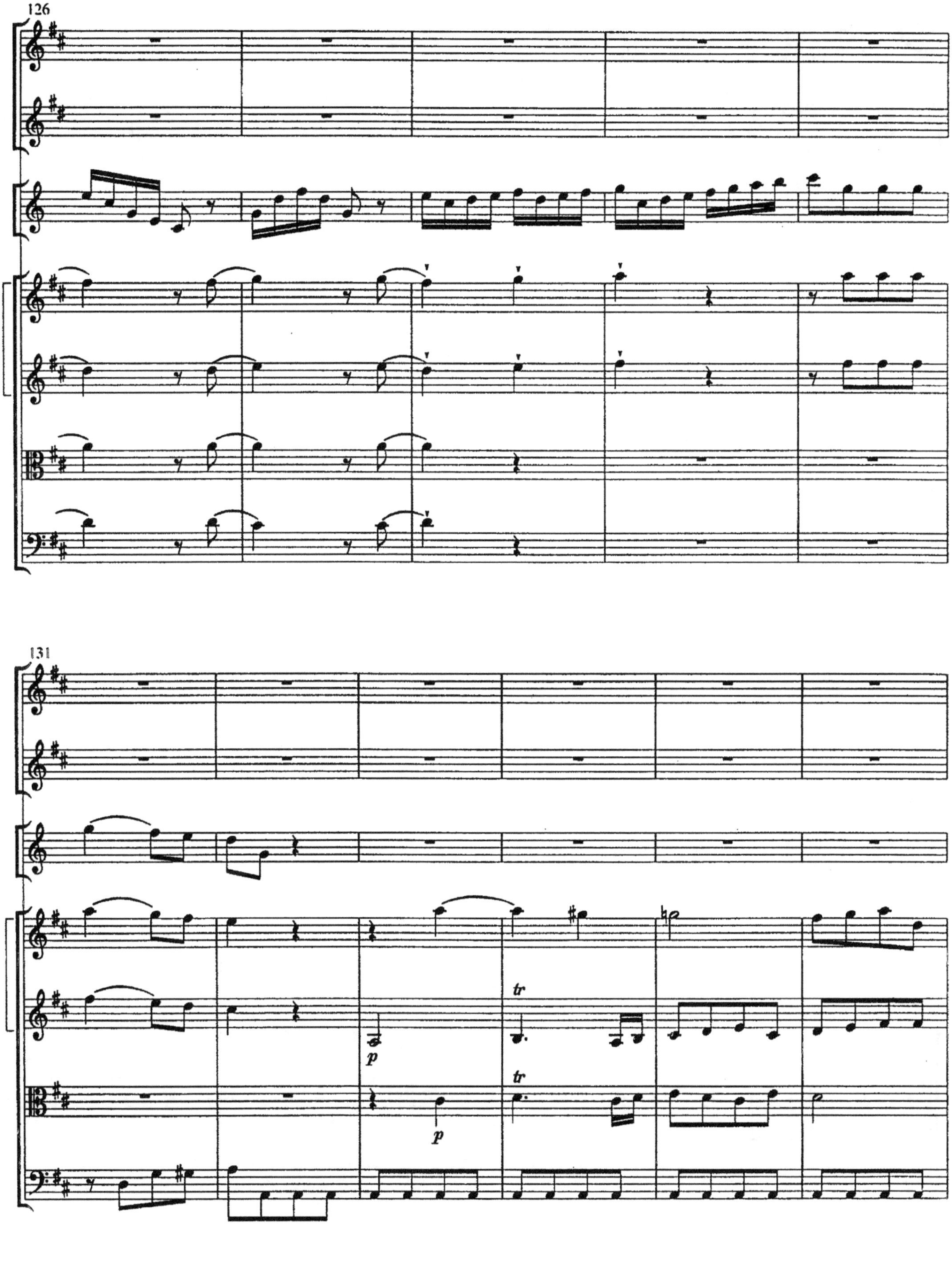
126
131
tr
p
tr
p

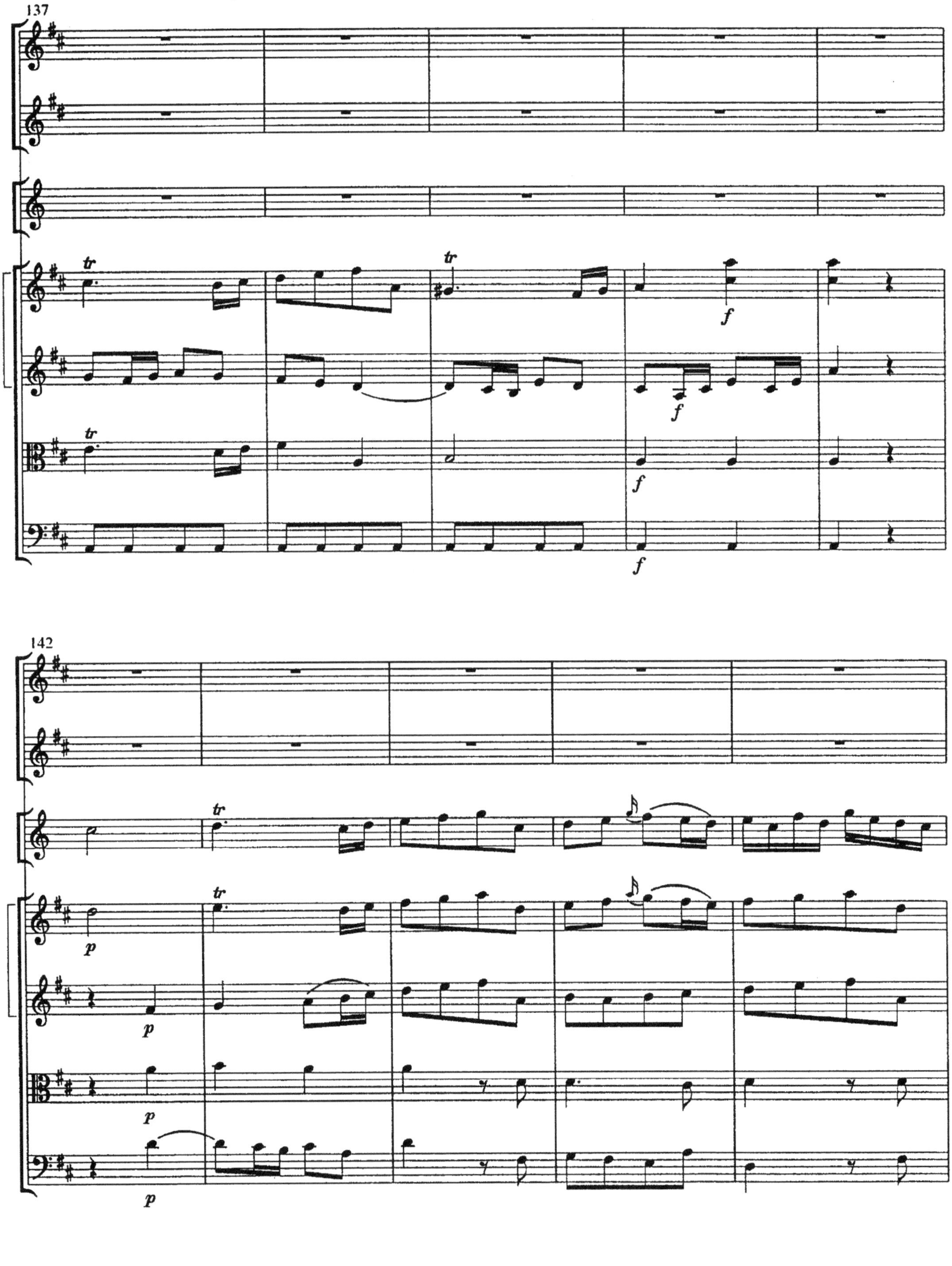
137
tr
tr
f
f
f
f
142
tr
tr
p
p
p
p

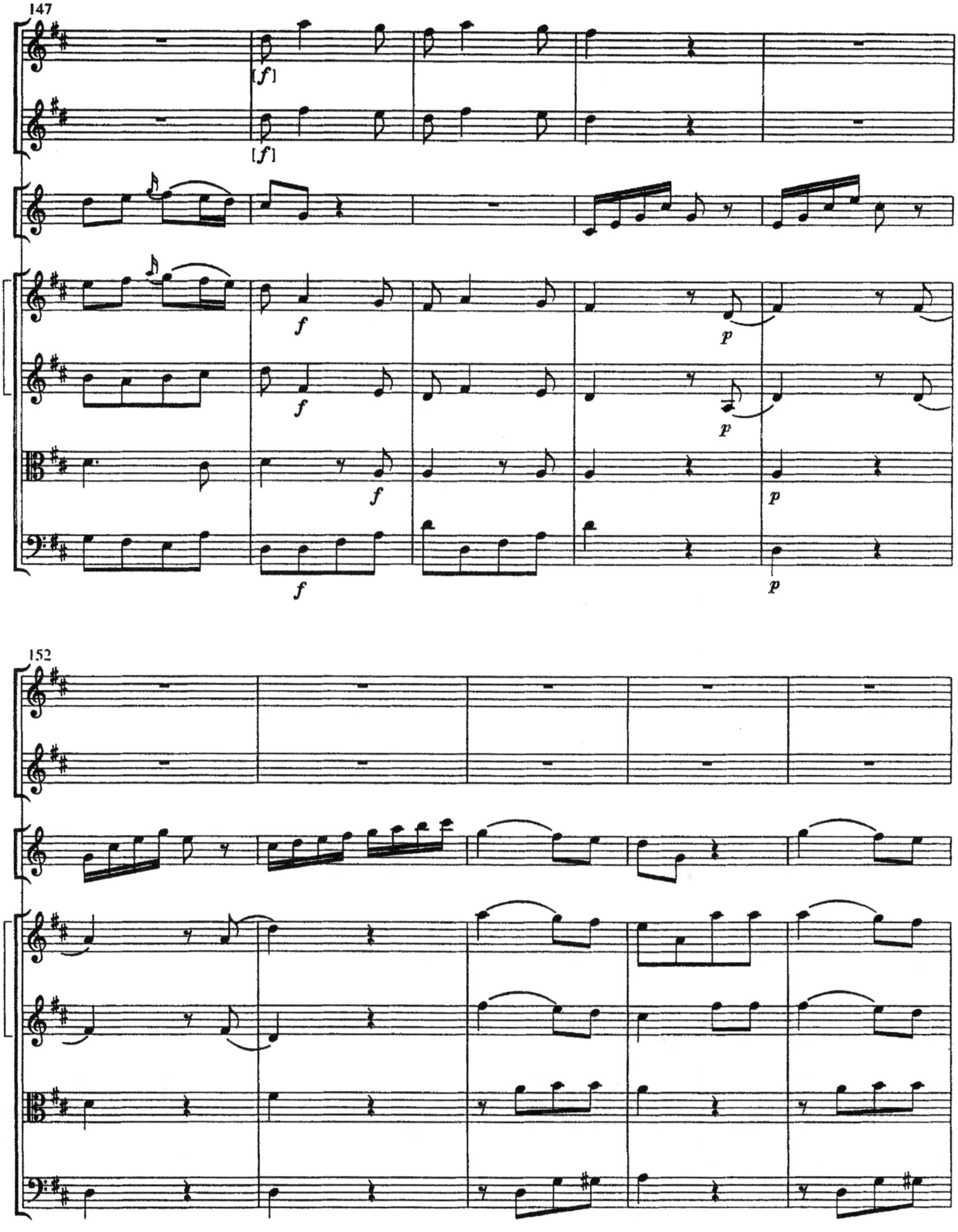
147
152

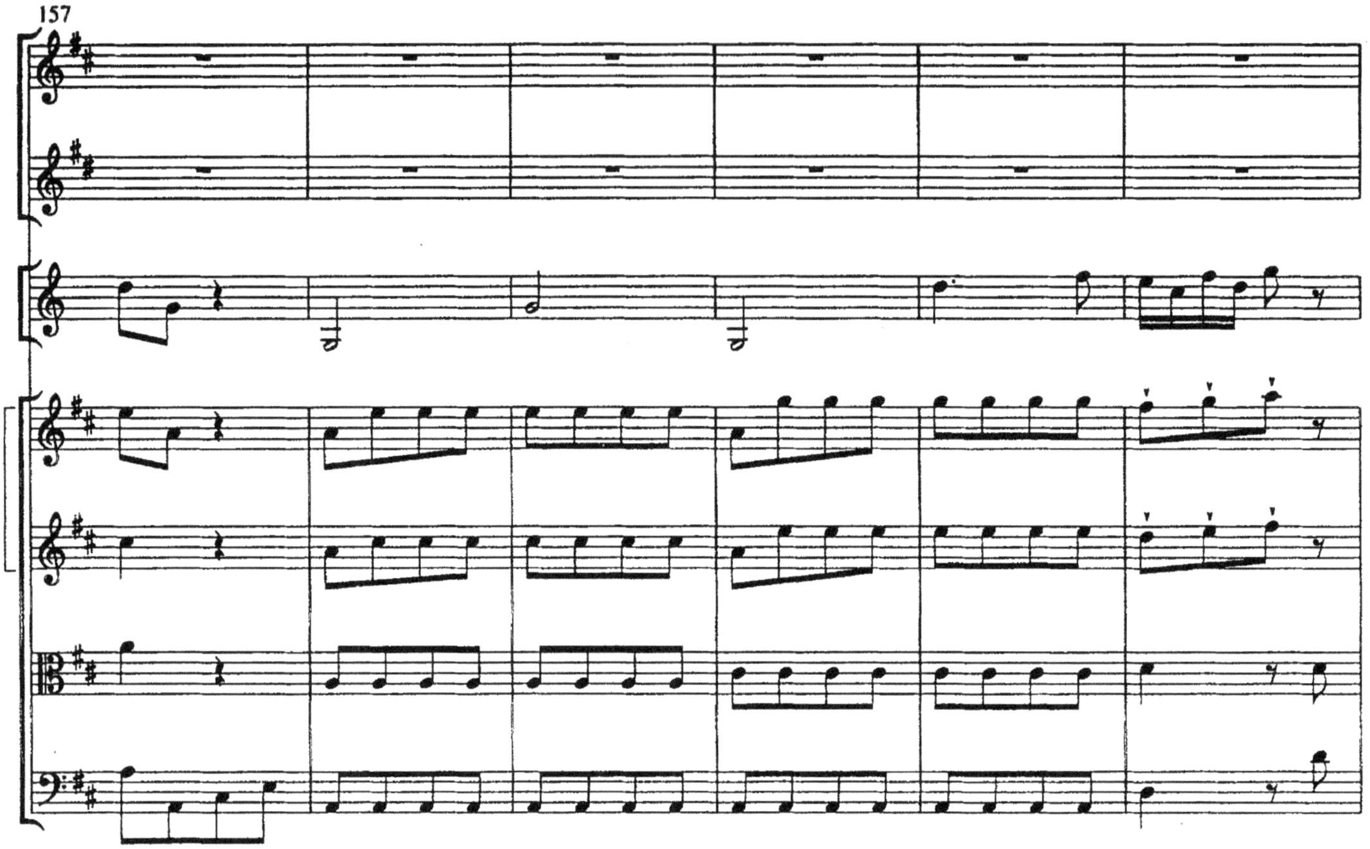
157

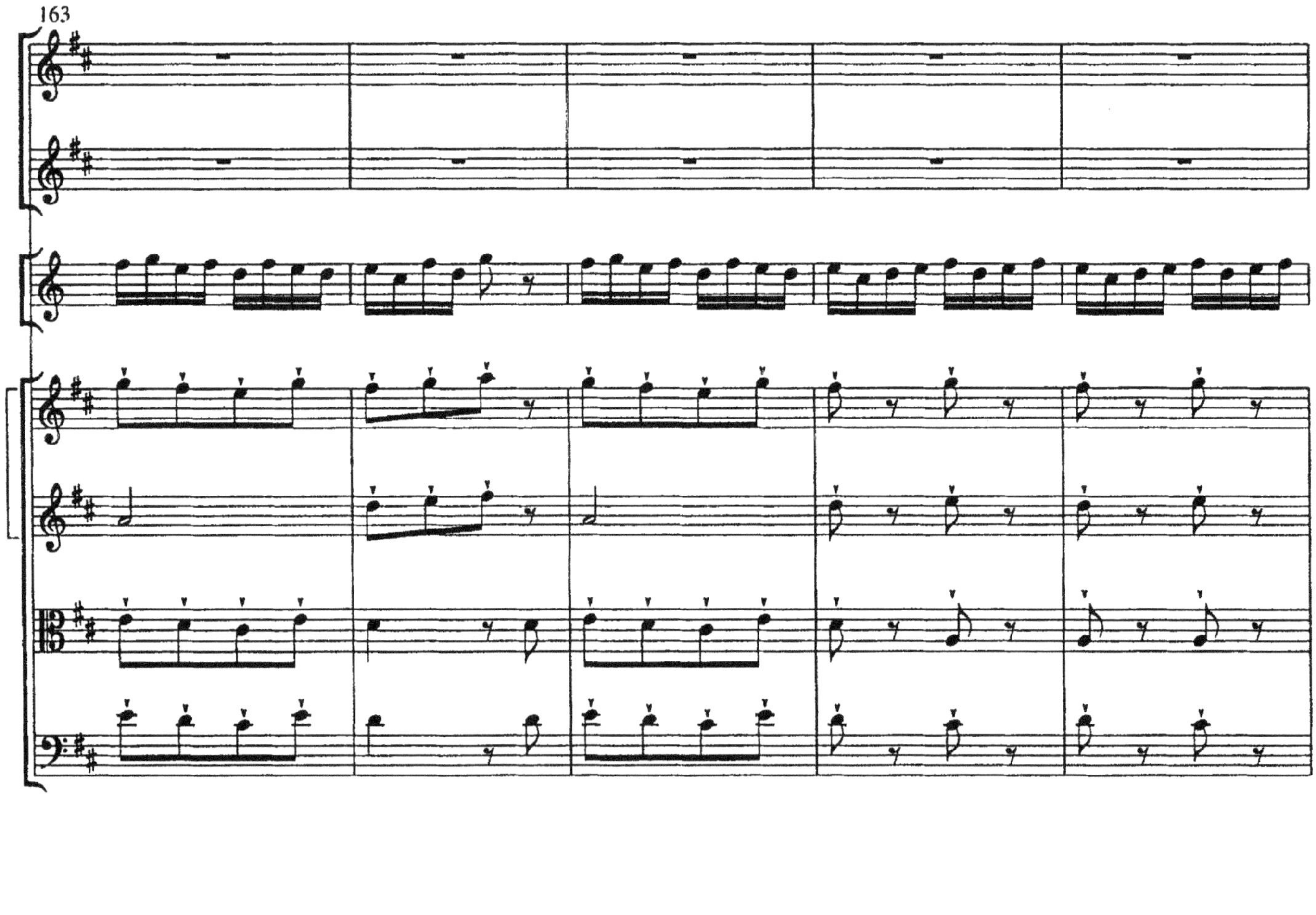
163

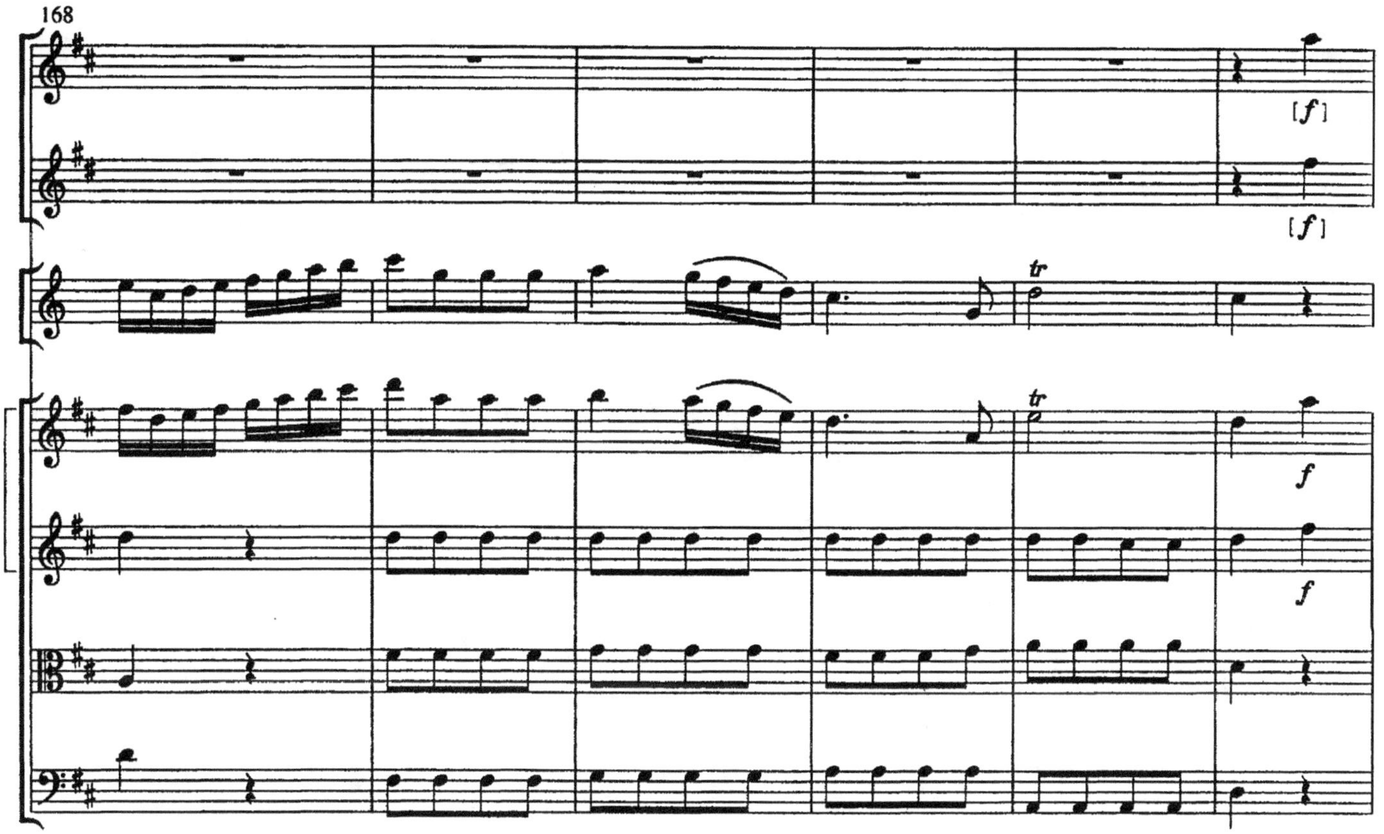
168
[f]
[f]
tr
tr
f
f

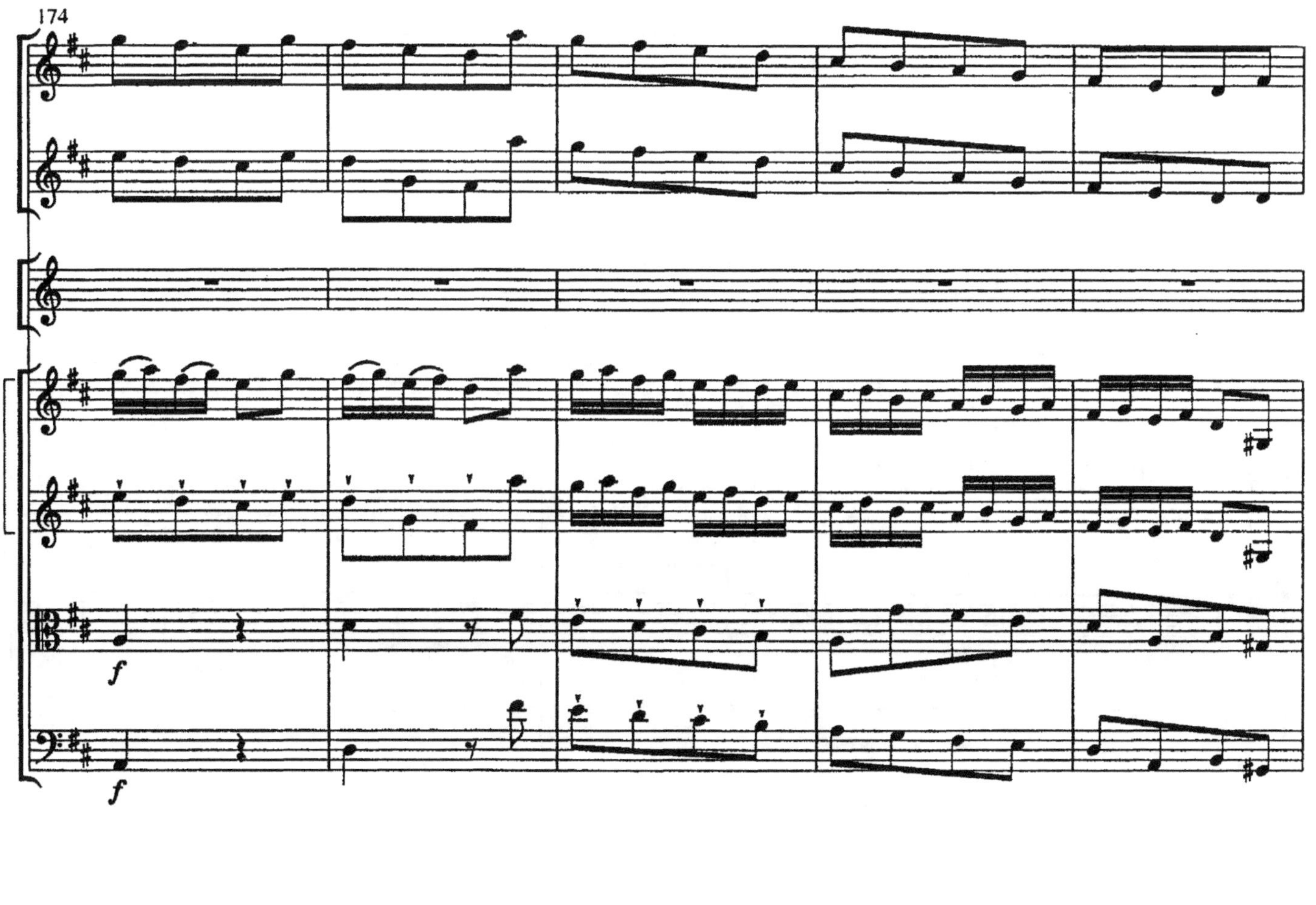
174
f
f

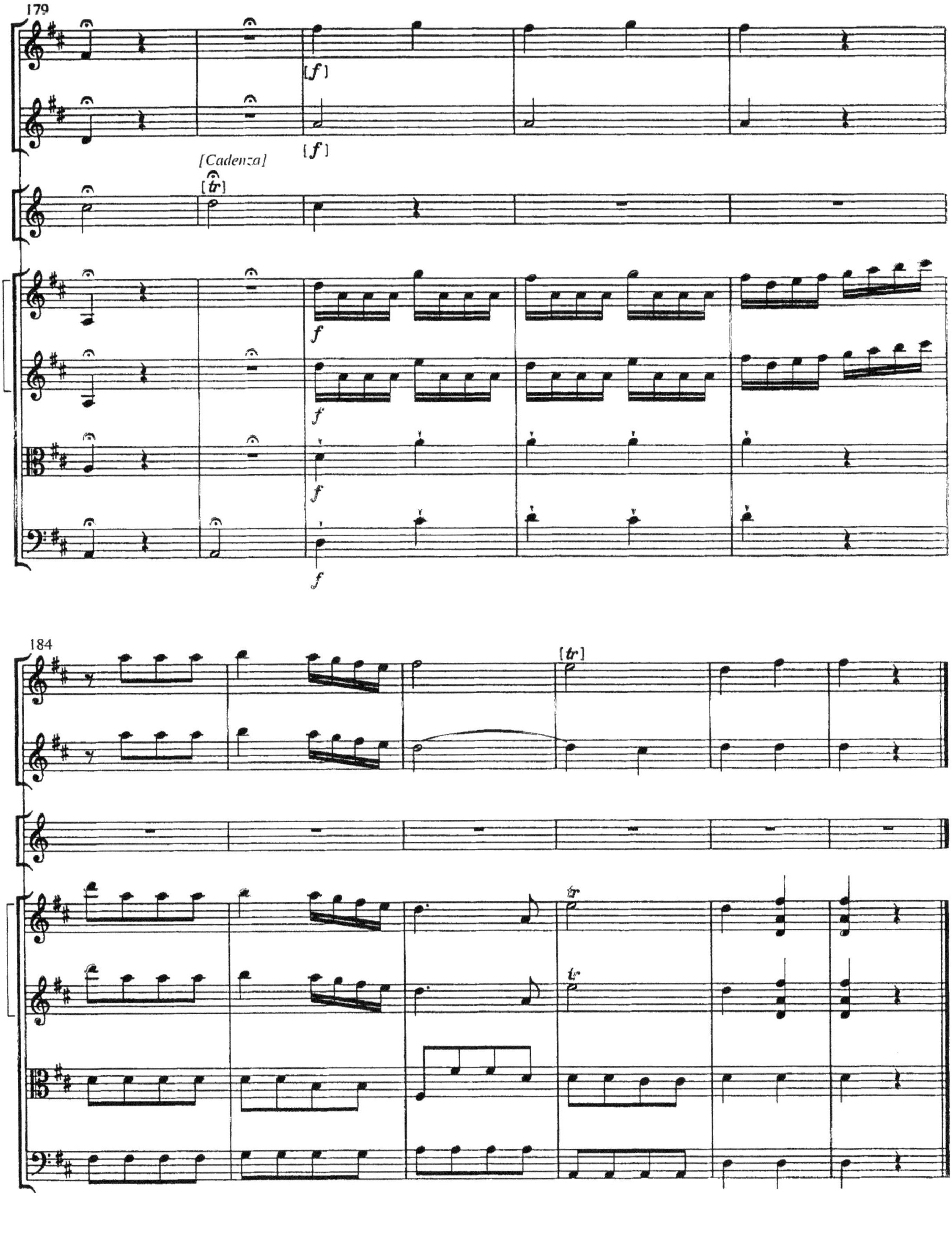
179
[Cadenza]
[tr]
[f]
f
184
tr

Concerto (No. 2)
for Horn and Orchestra

Joseph Haydn (H. VIId:4)
Practical Edition by Clark McAlister

* Horn Solo: Play this and all similar figures in this movement as ♩ ♫ to agree with written orchestra rhythm.

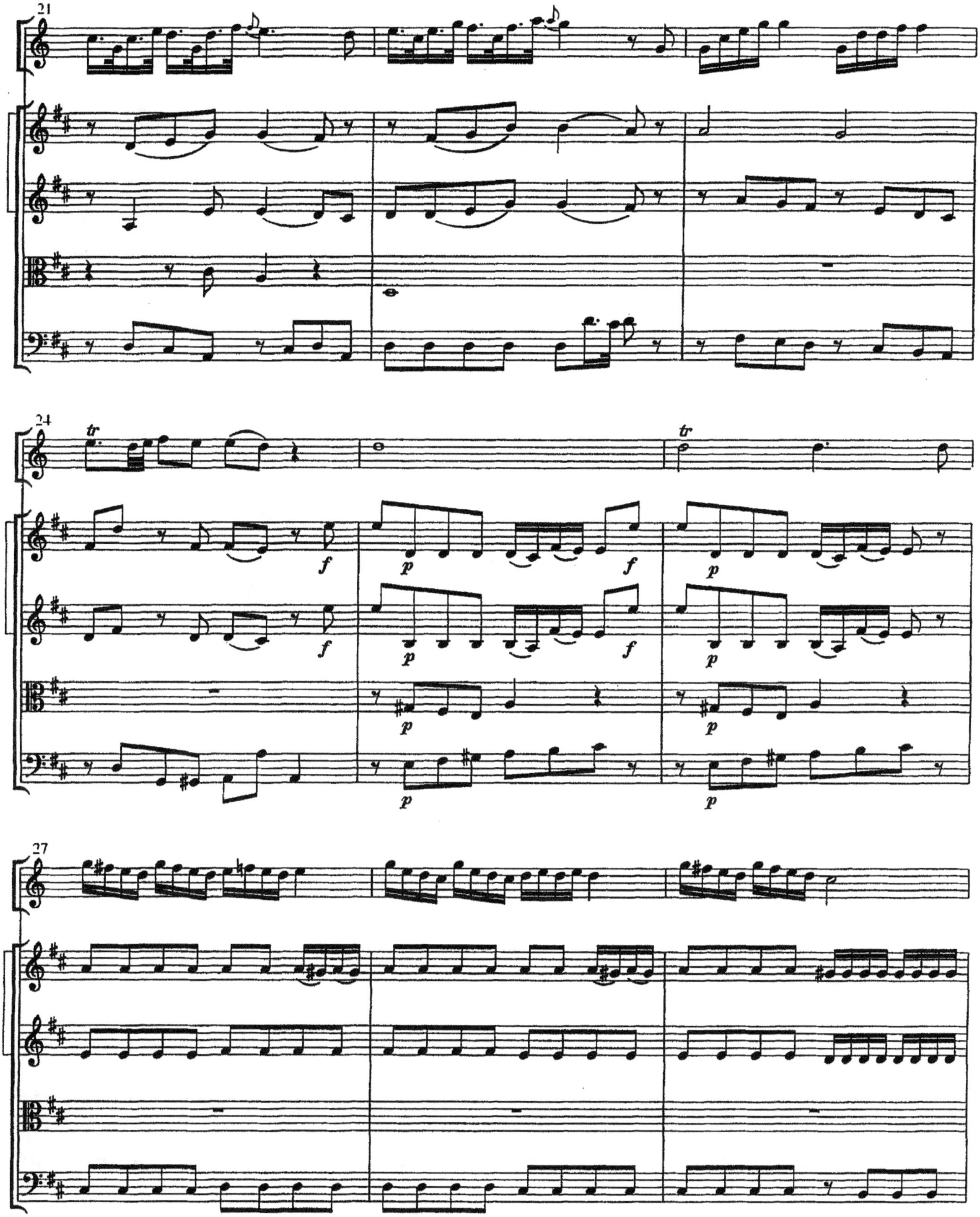
21
24
tr
f
p
27

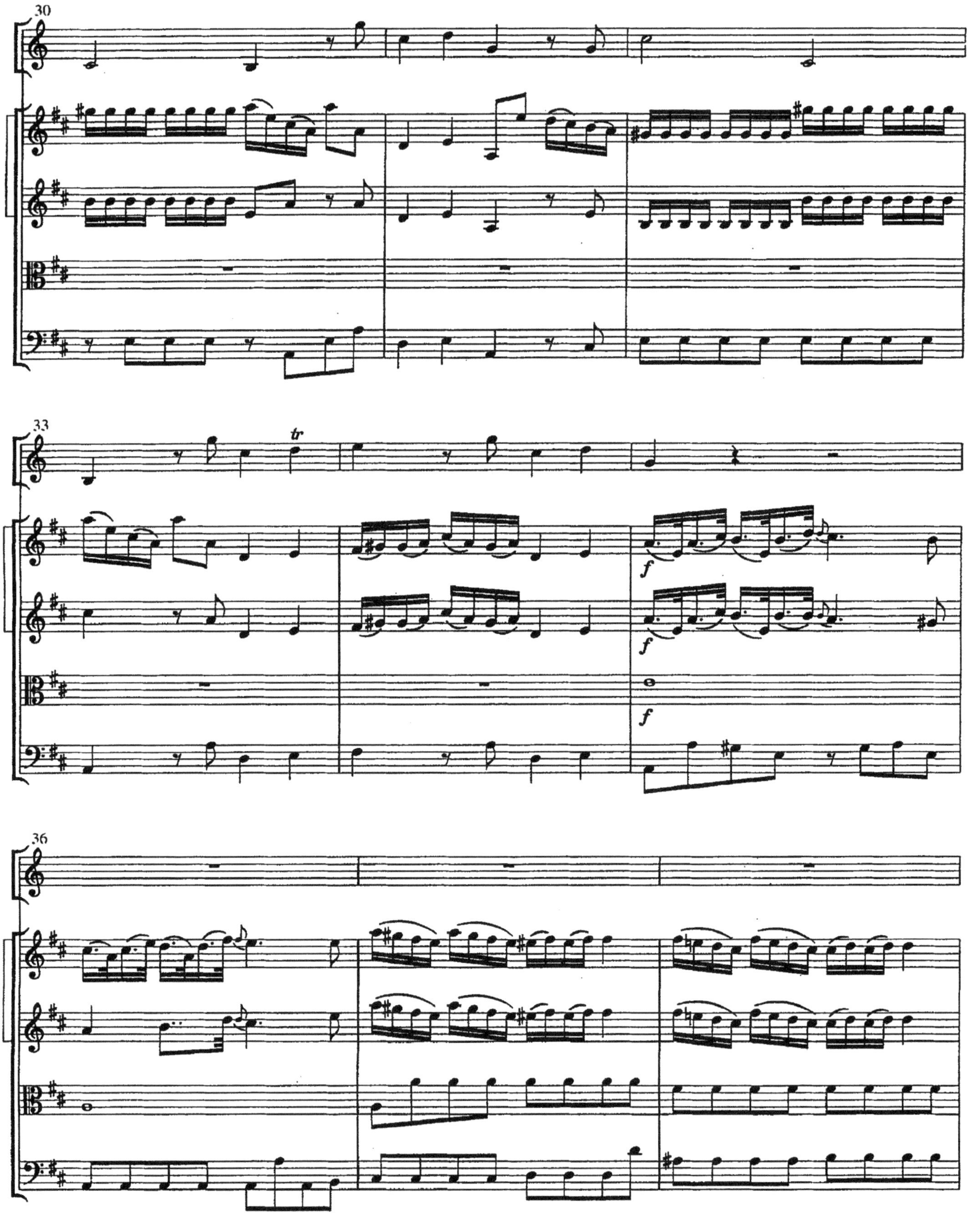
30
33
tr
f
f
f
36

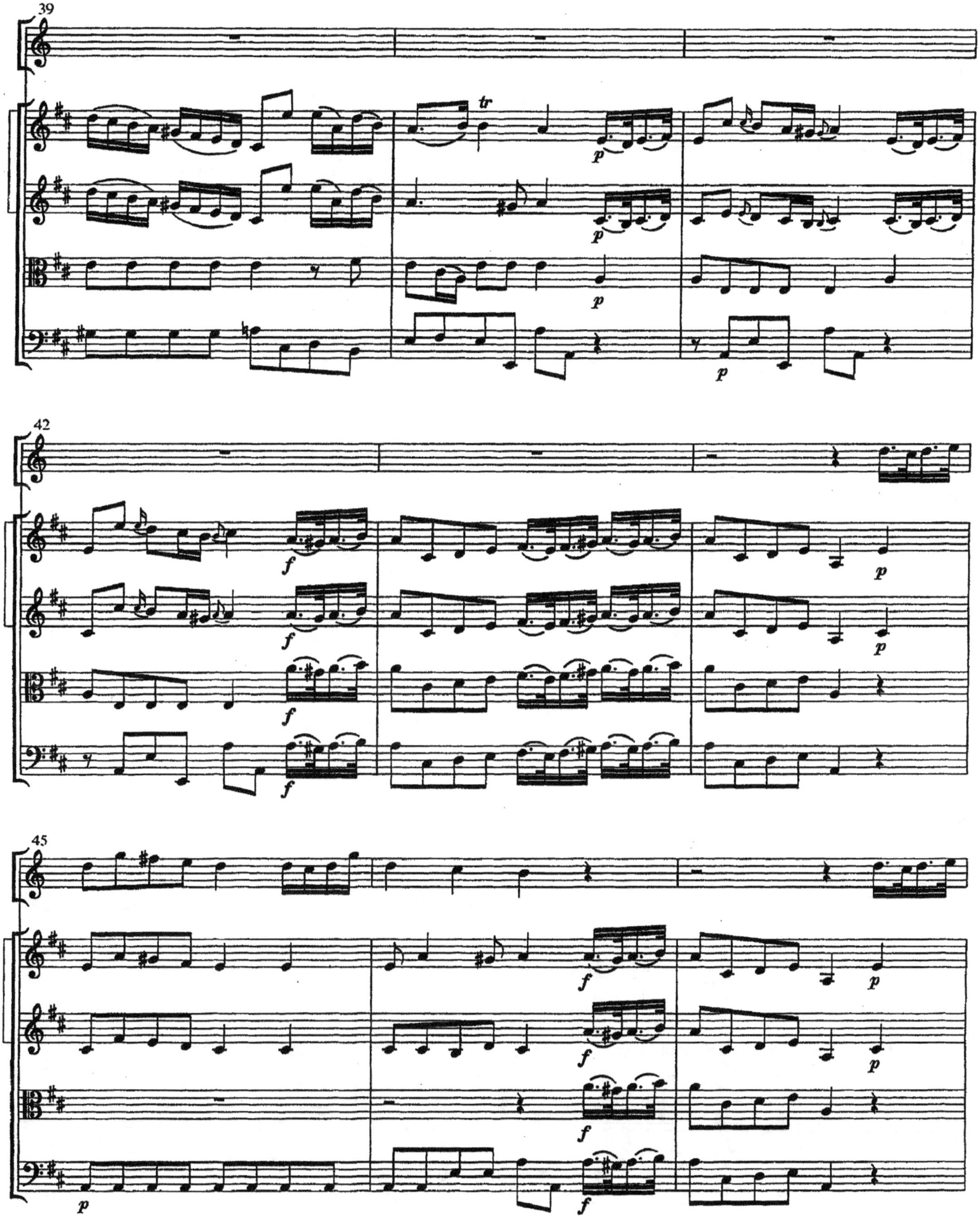
39
tr
p
p
p
p
42
f
f
f
f
p
p
45
p
f
f
f
f
p
p

54

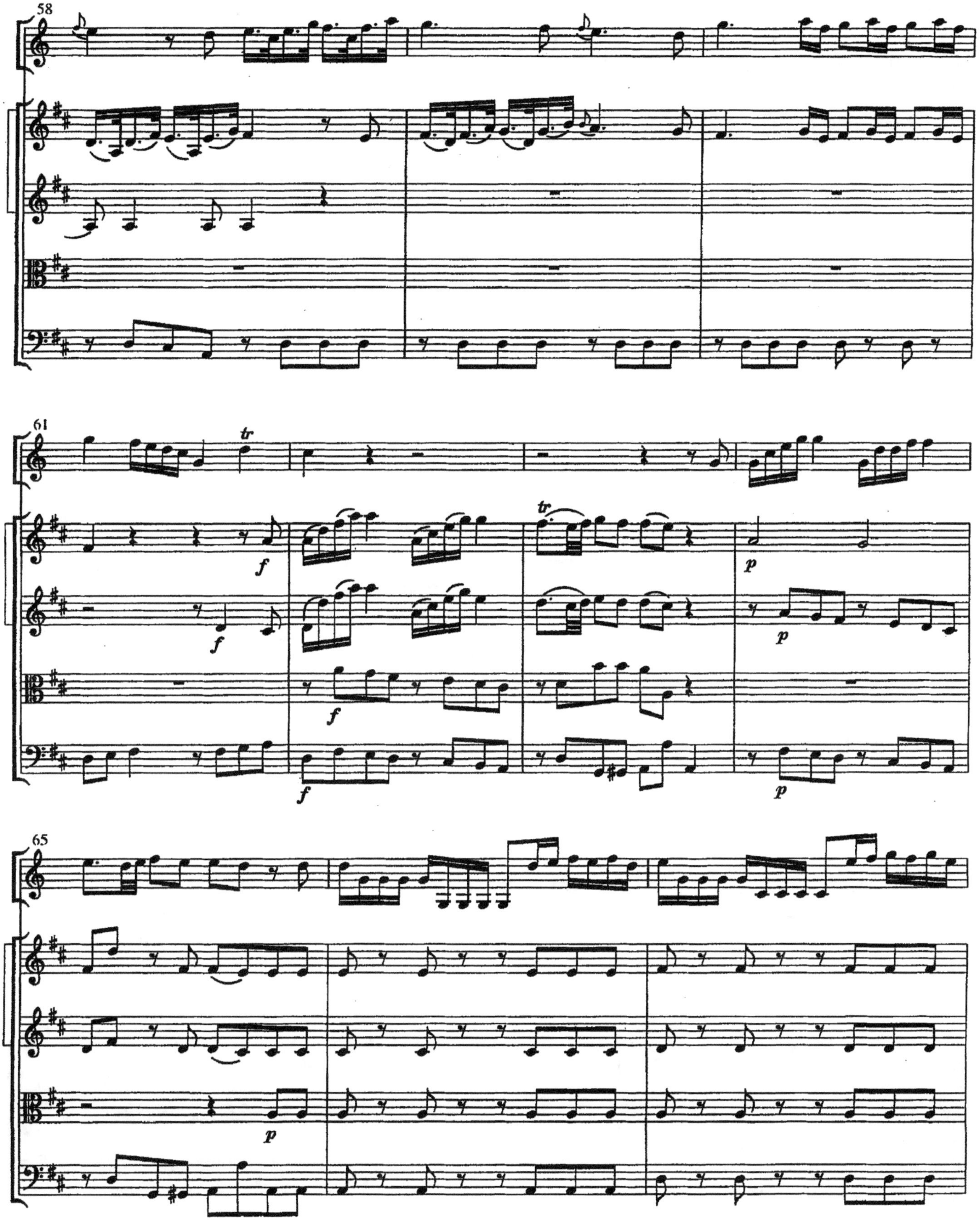
58
tr
f
f
f
f
p
p
p
61
65
p

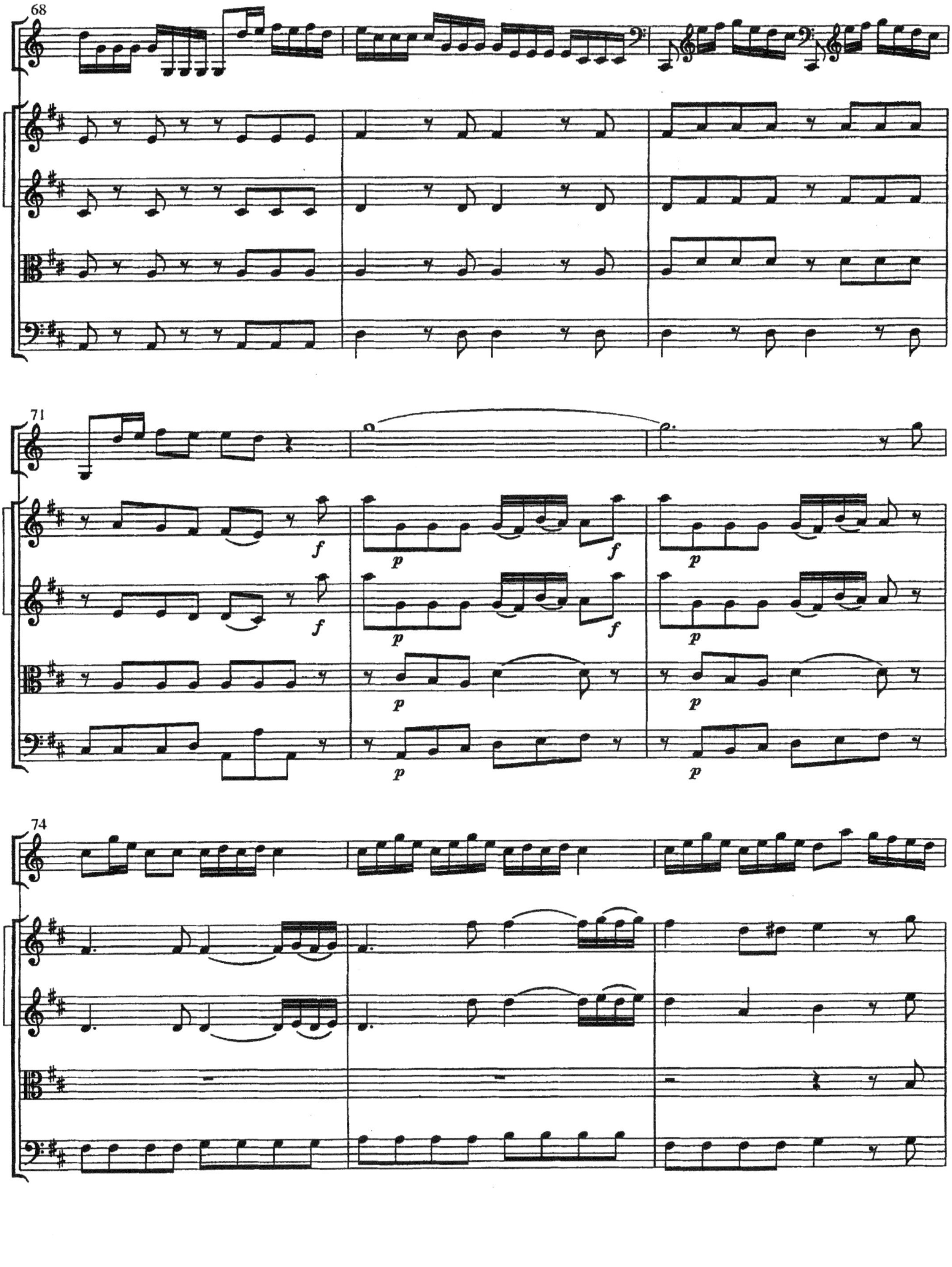
68
71
f
p
74

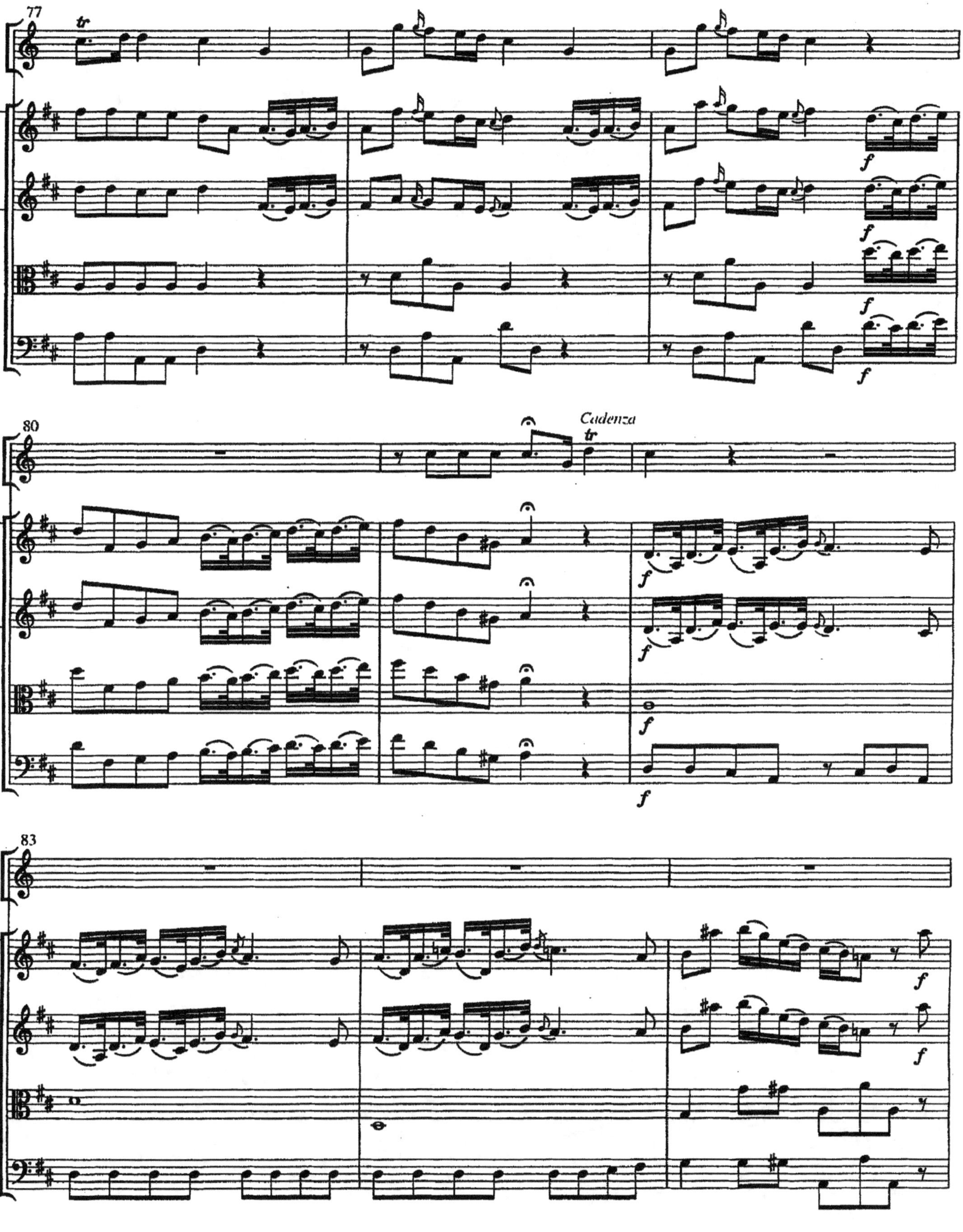
77
tr
f
80
Cadenza
tr
f
83
f

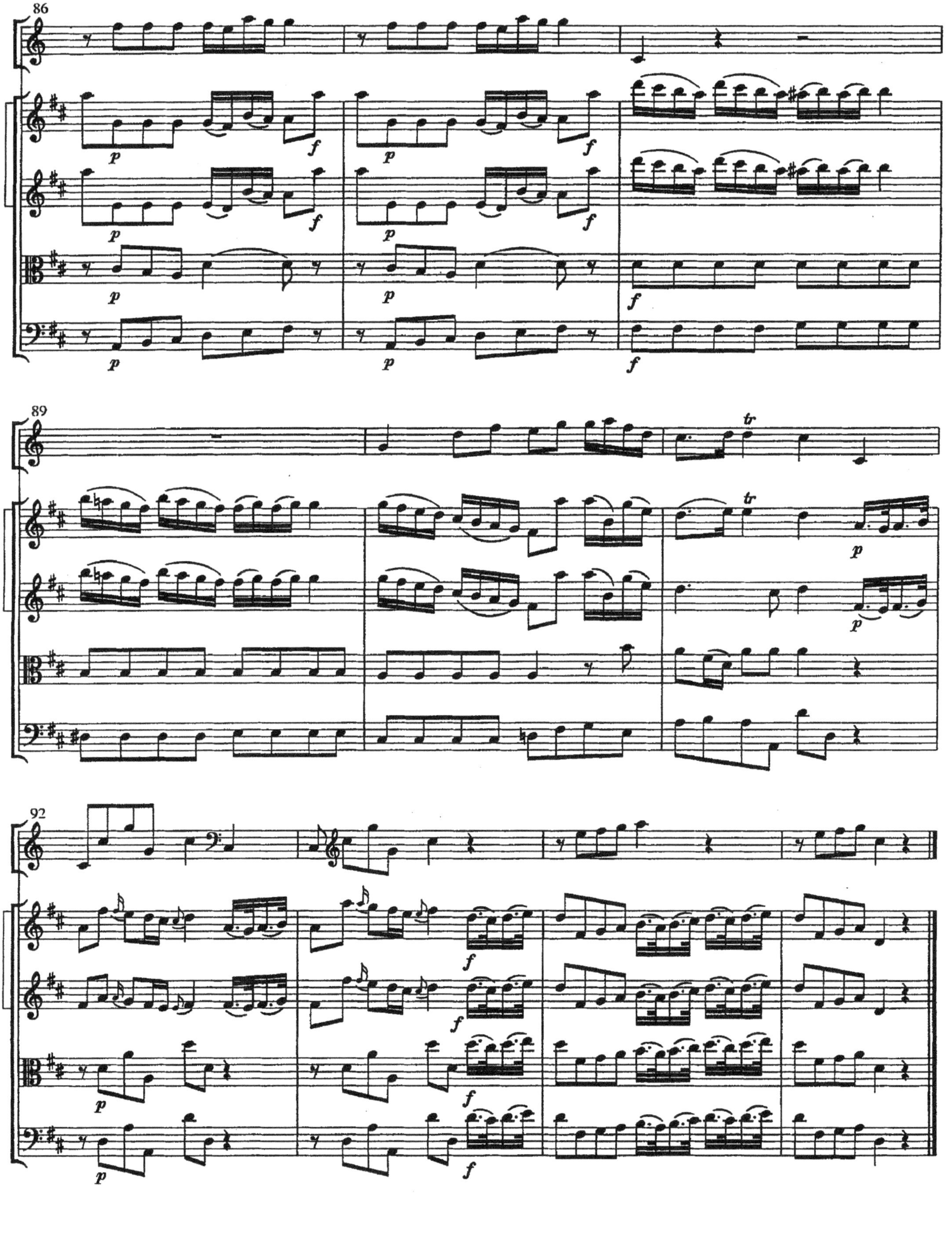
86
89
92

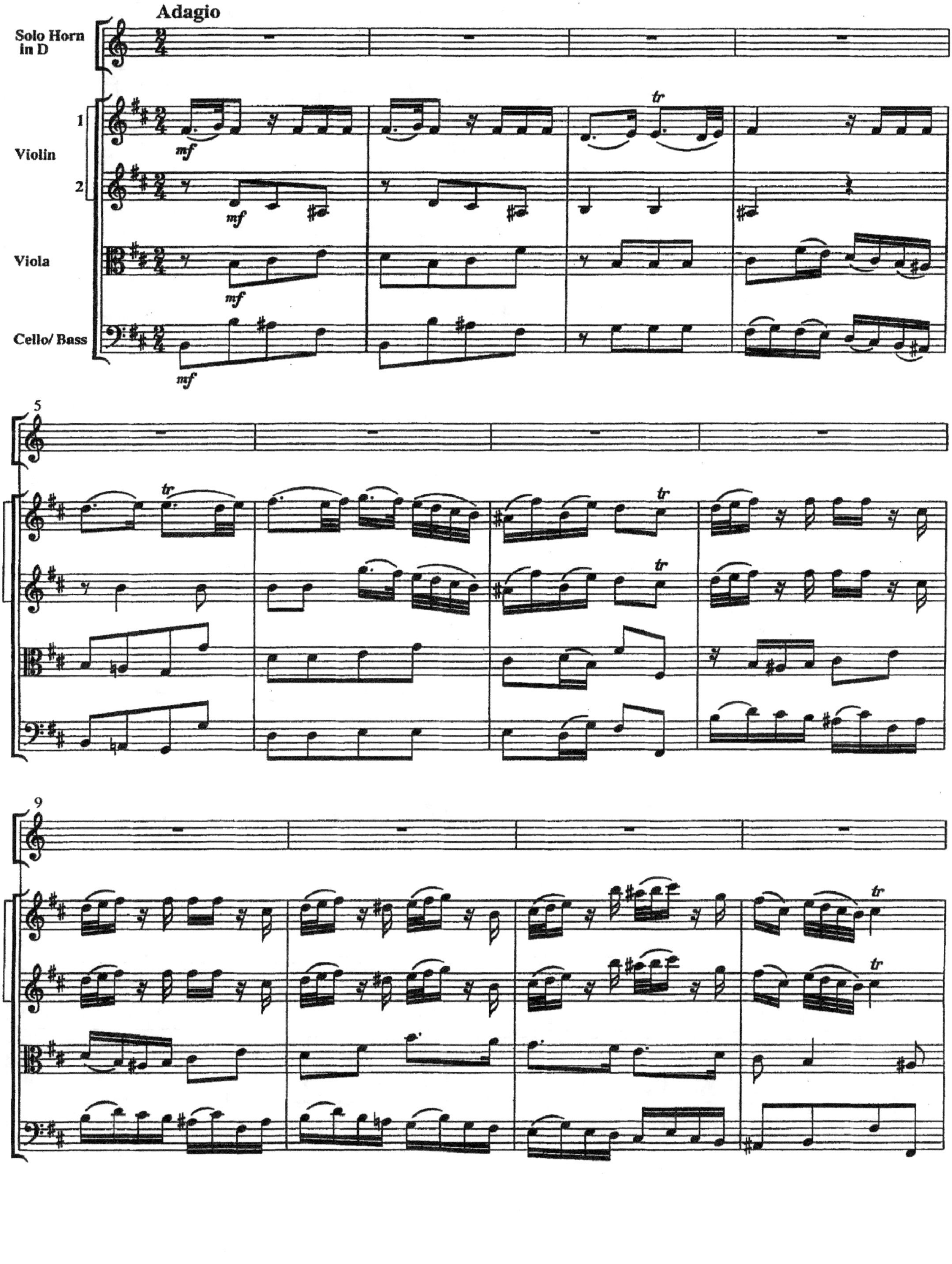
Adagio
Solo Horn in D
Violin
1
2
Viola
Cello/ Bass
mf
tr
5
9

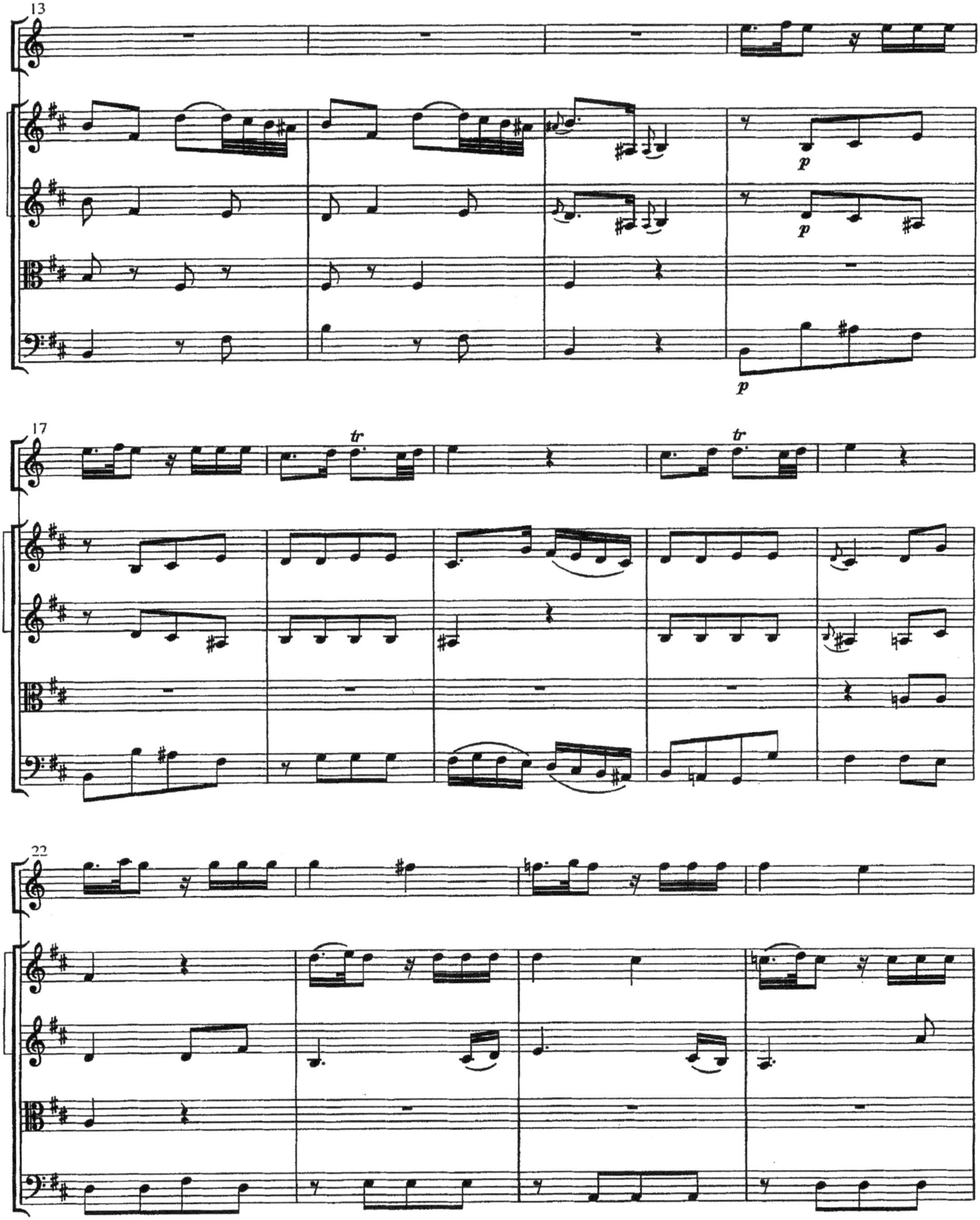
13
p
p
p
17
tr
tr
22

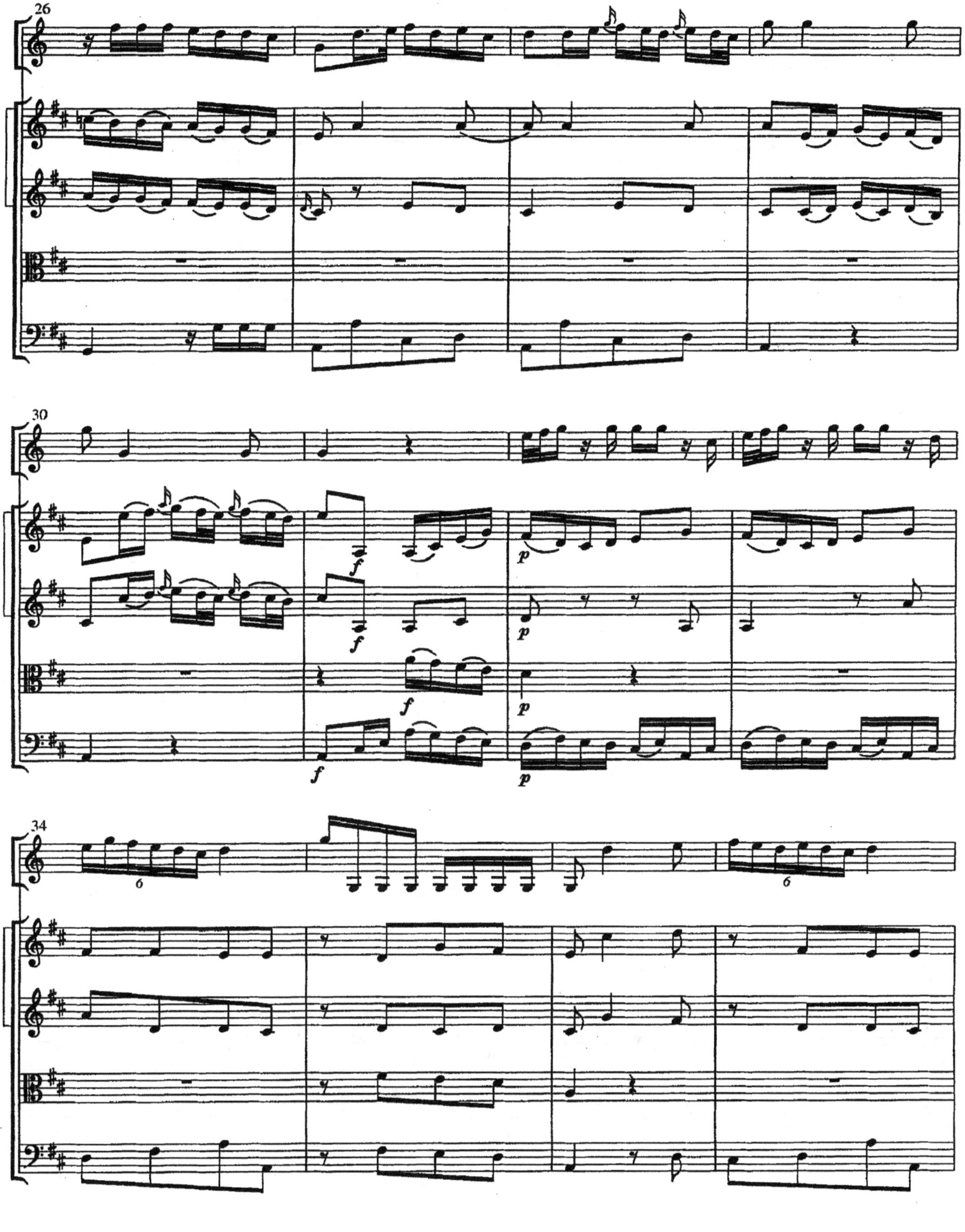
26
30
f
p
34
6

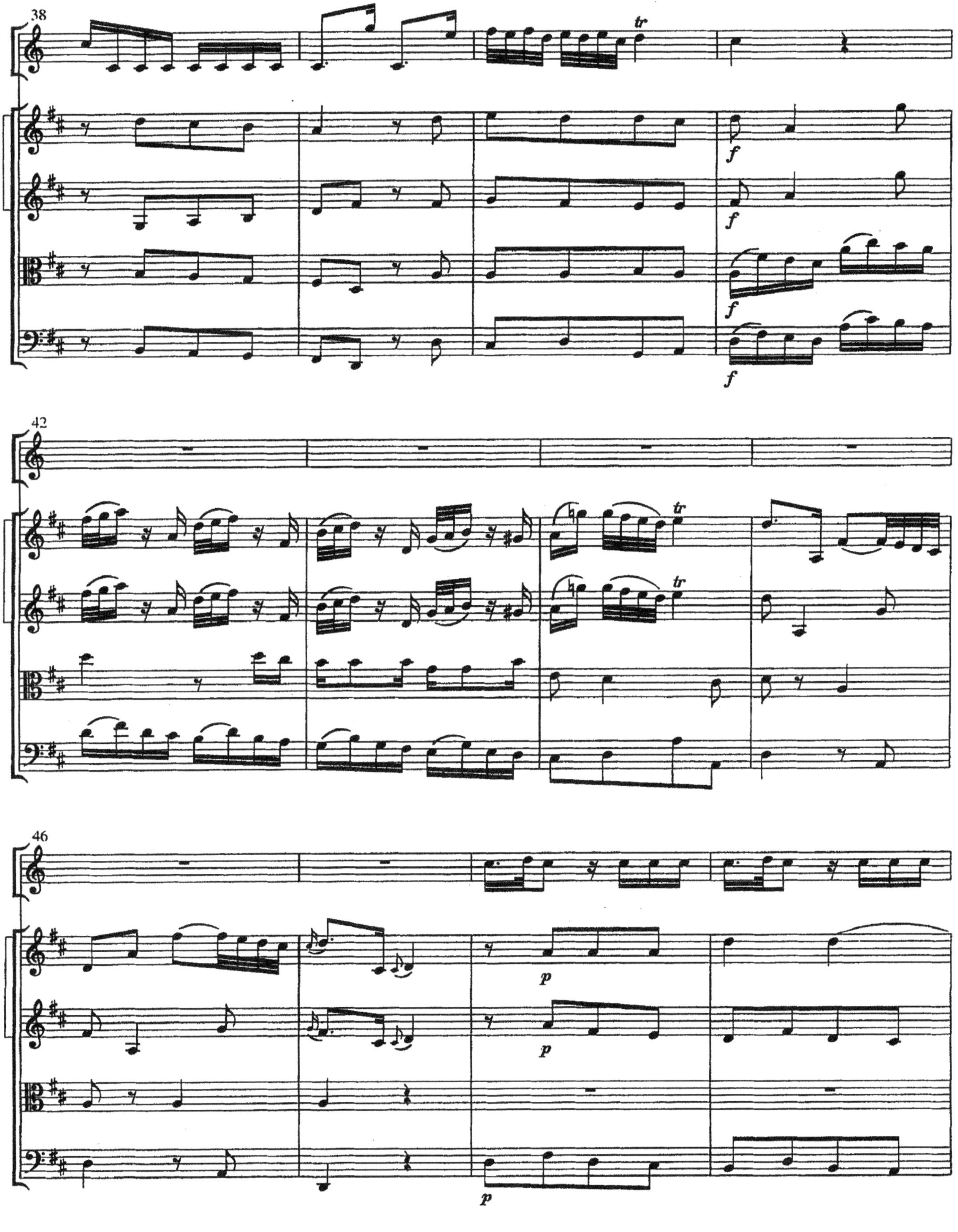
38
tr
f
f
f
f
42
tr
tr
46
p
p
p

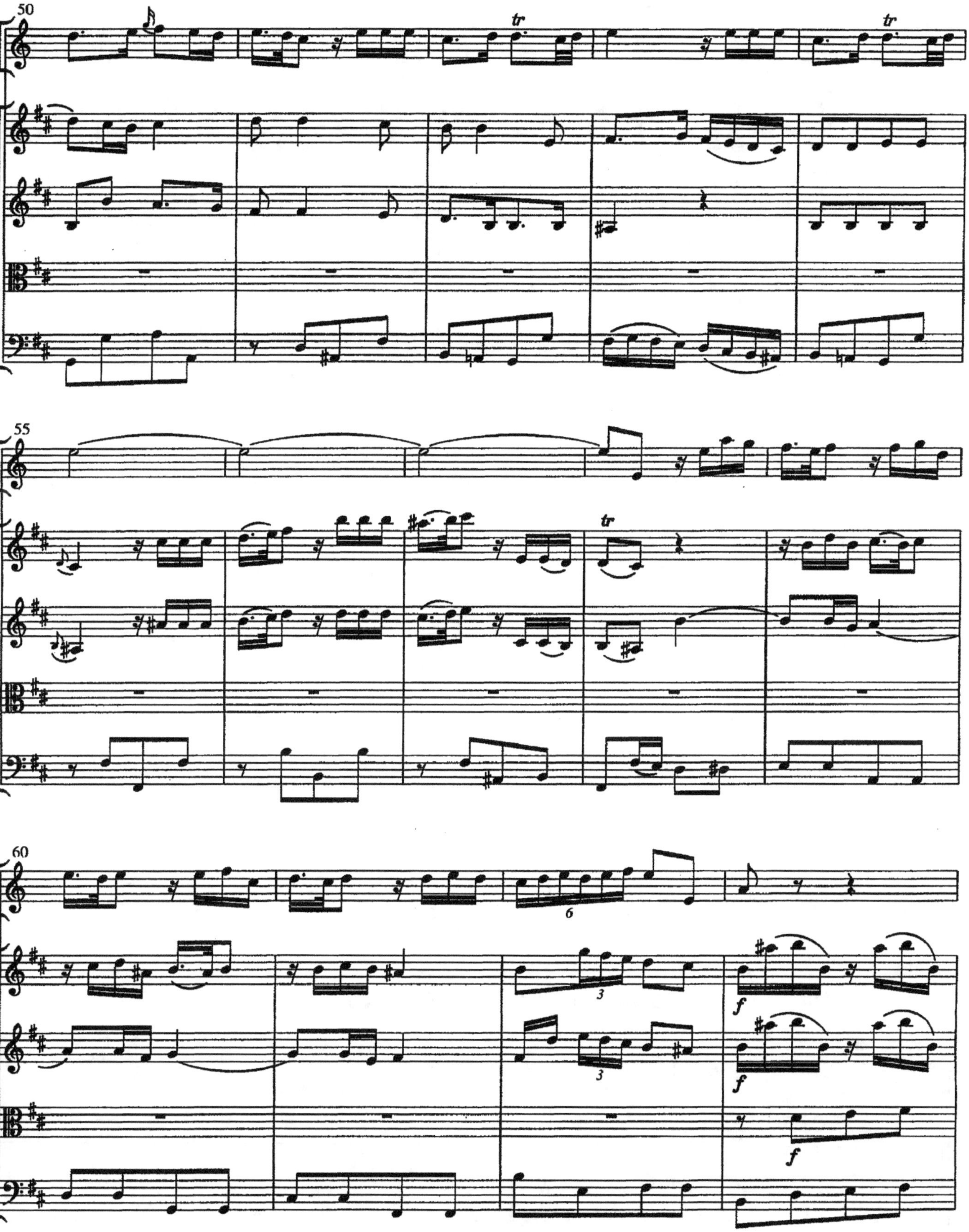
50
55
60

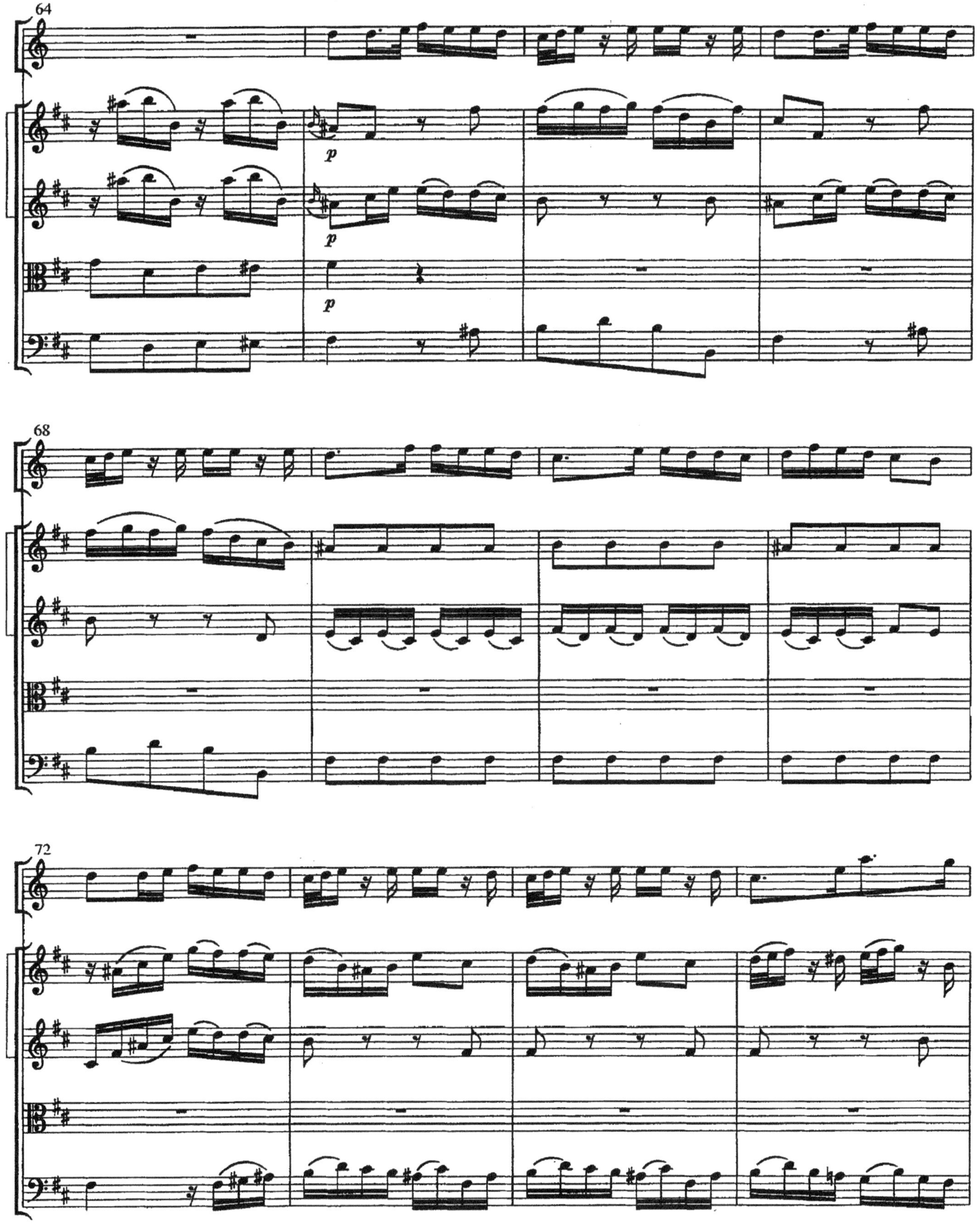
64
p
p
p
68
72

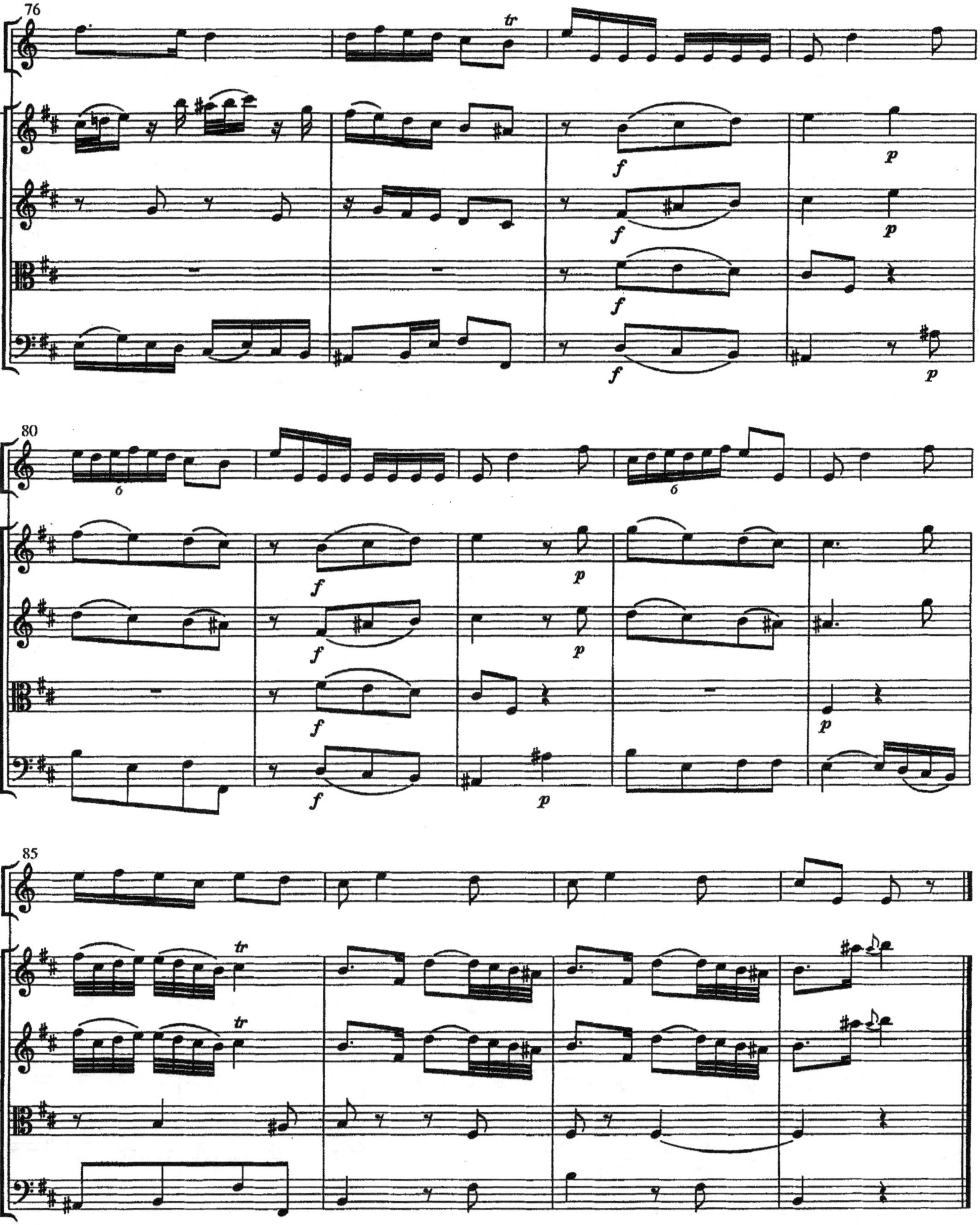
76
tr
f
p
80
6
85
tr

66

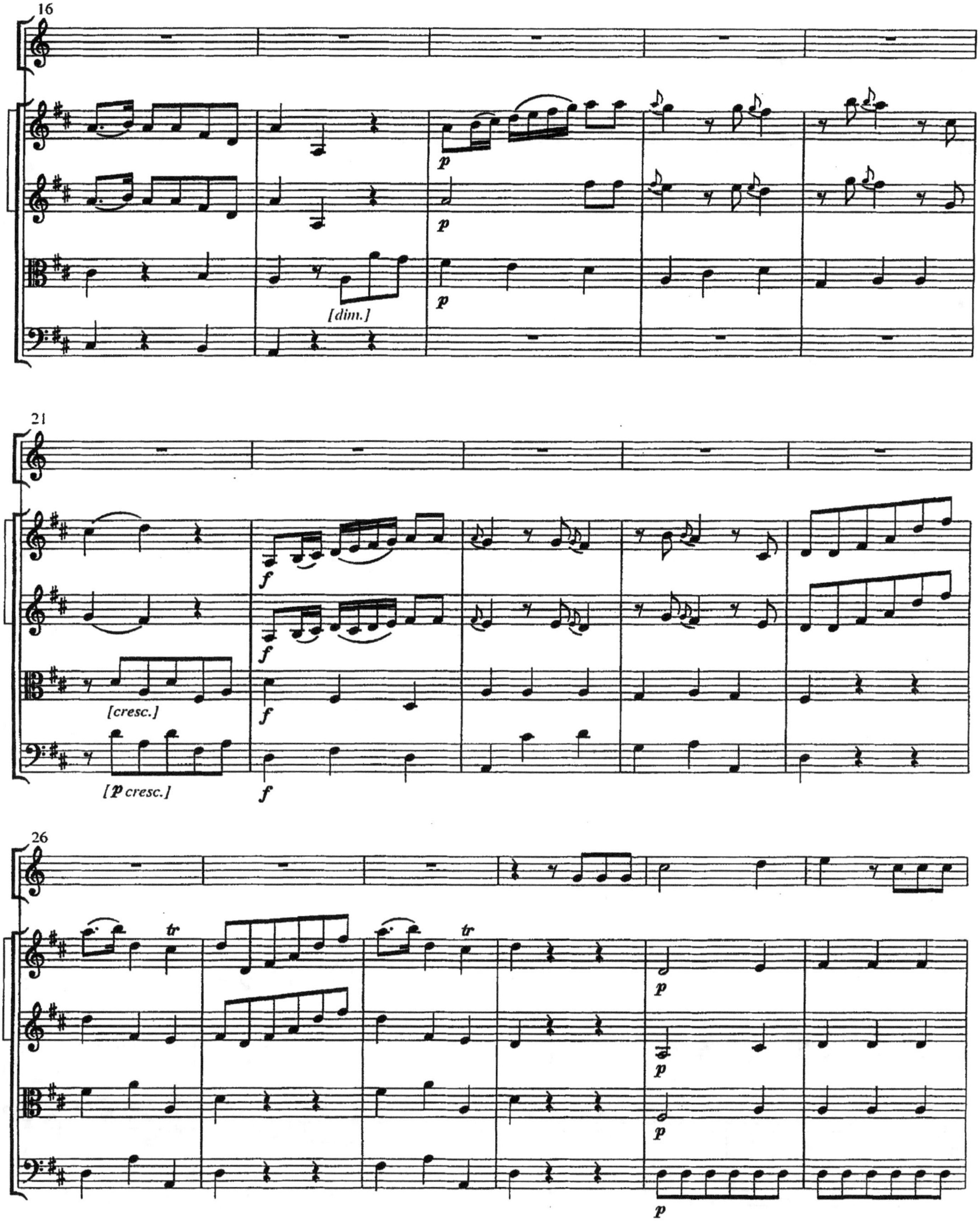
16
p
p
p
[dim.]
21
f
f
f
f
[cresc.]
[p cresc.]
26
tr
tr
p
p
p
p

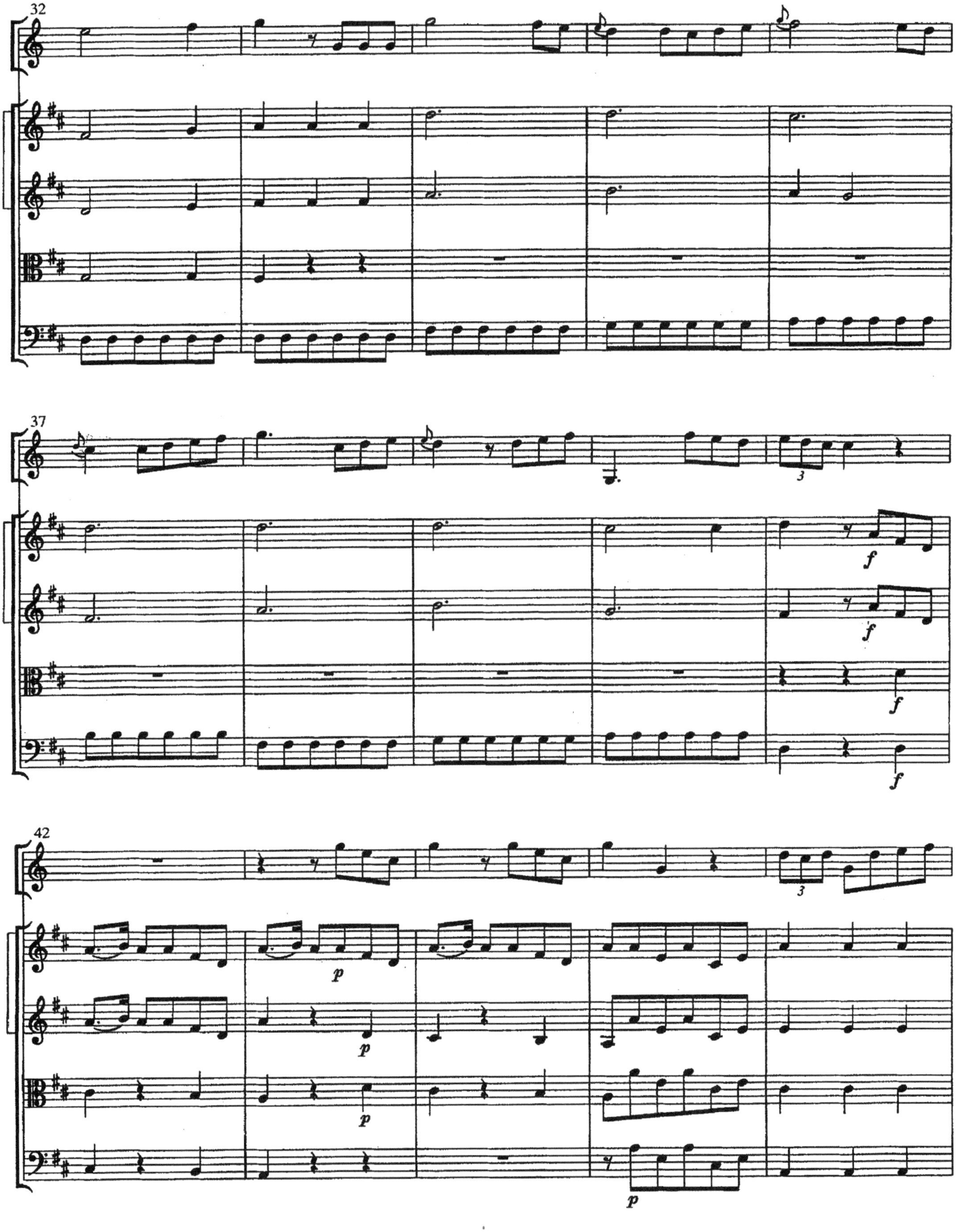
32
37
42

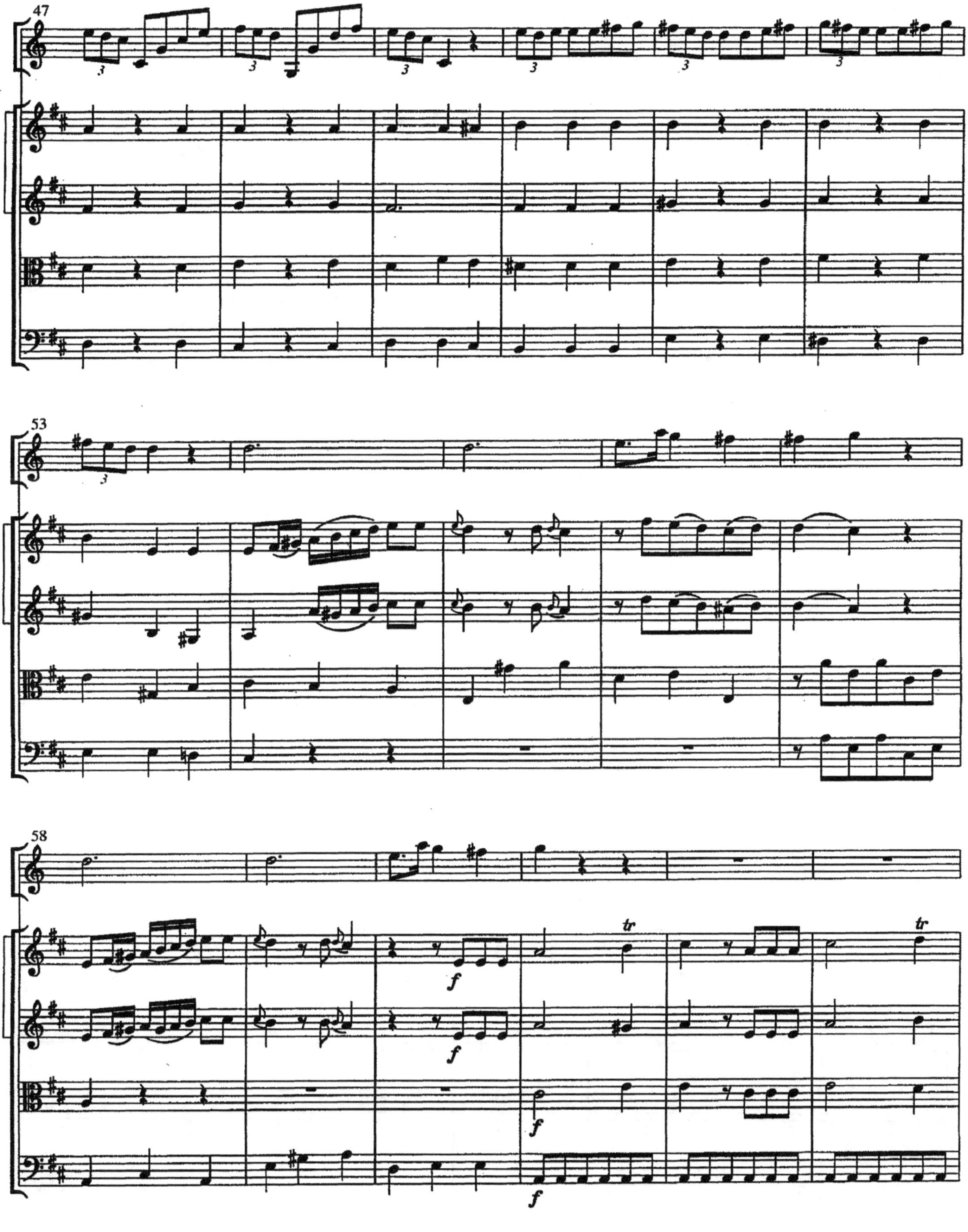
47
3
3
3
3
3
3
53
3
58
tr
tr
f
f
f
f

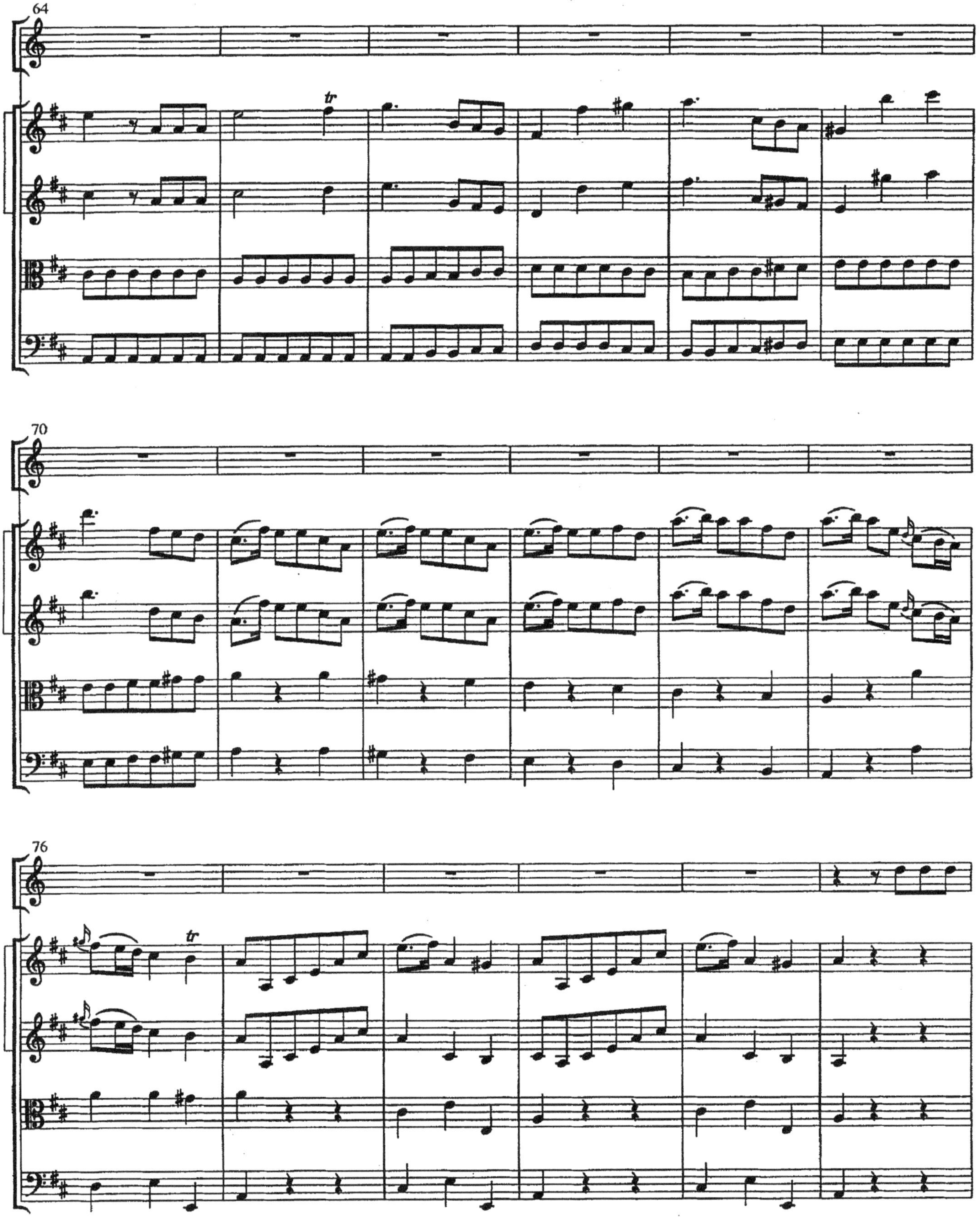
64
70
76

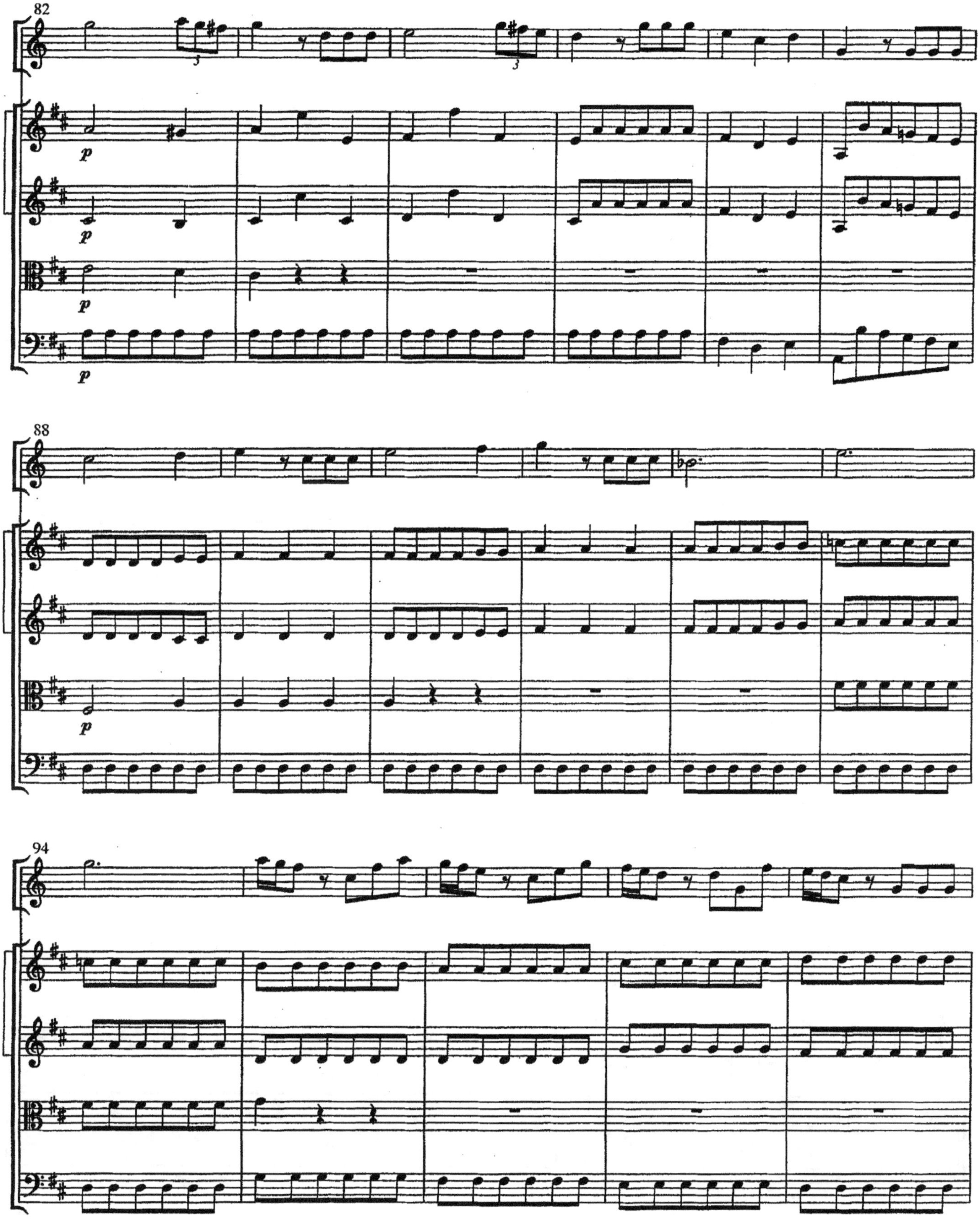
82
88
94

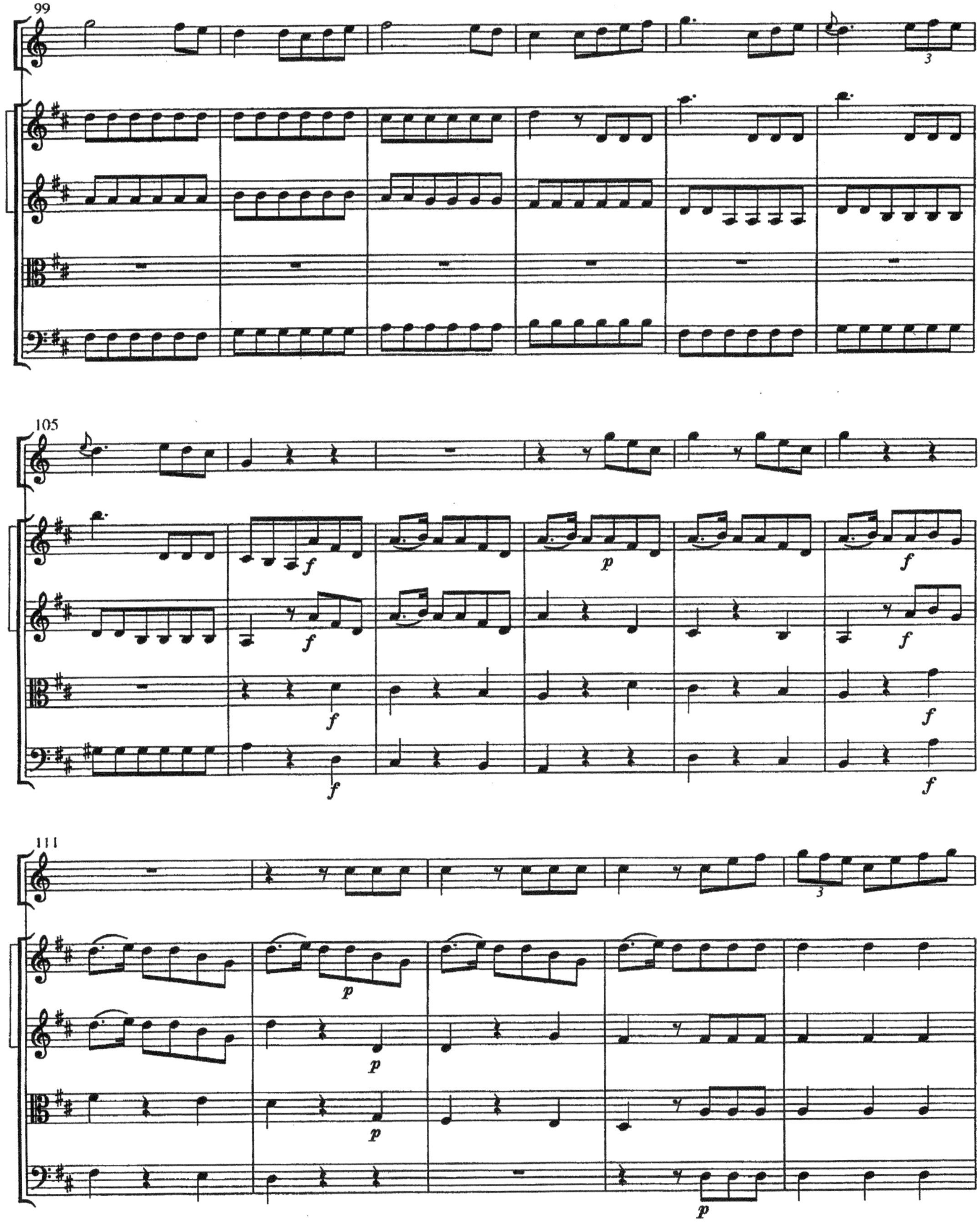
99
105
111

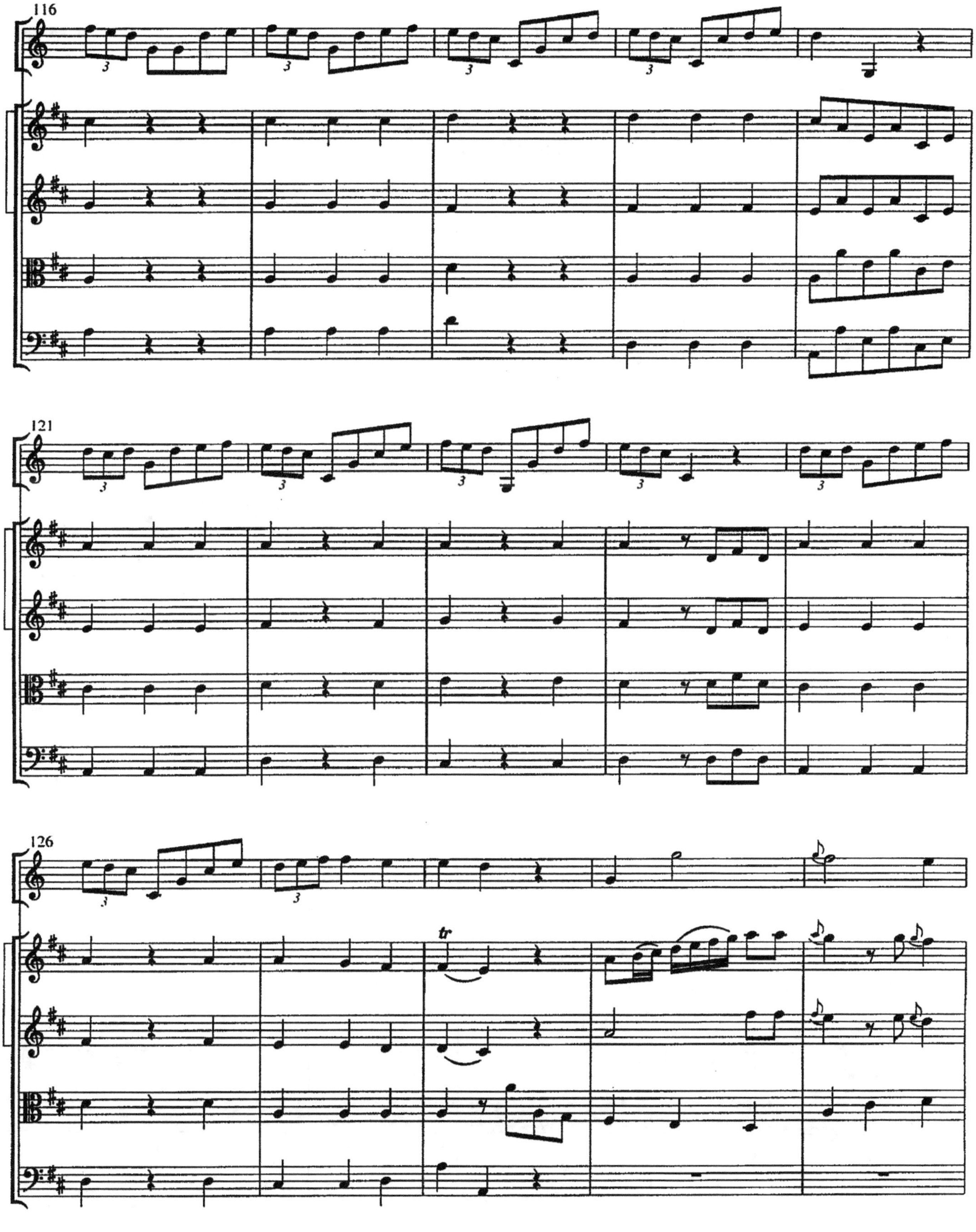
116
121
126
tr

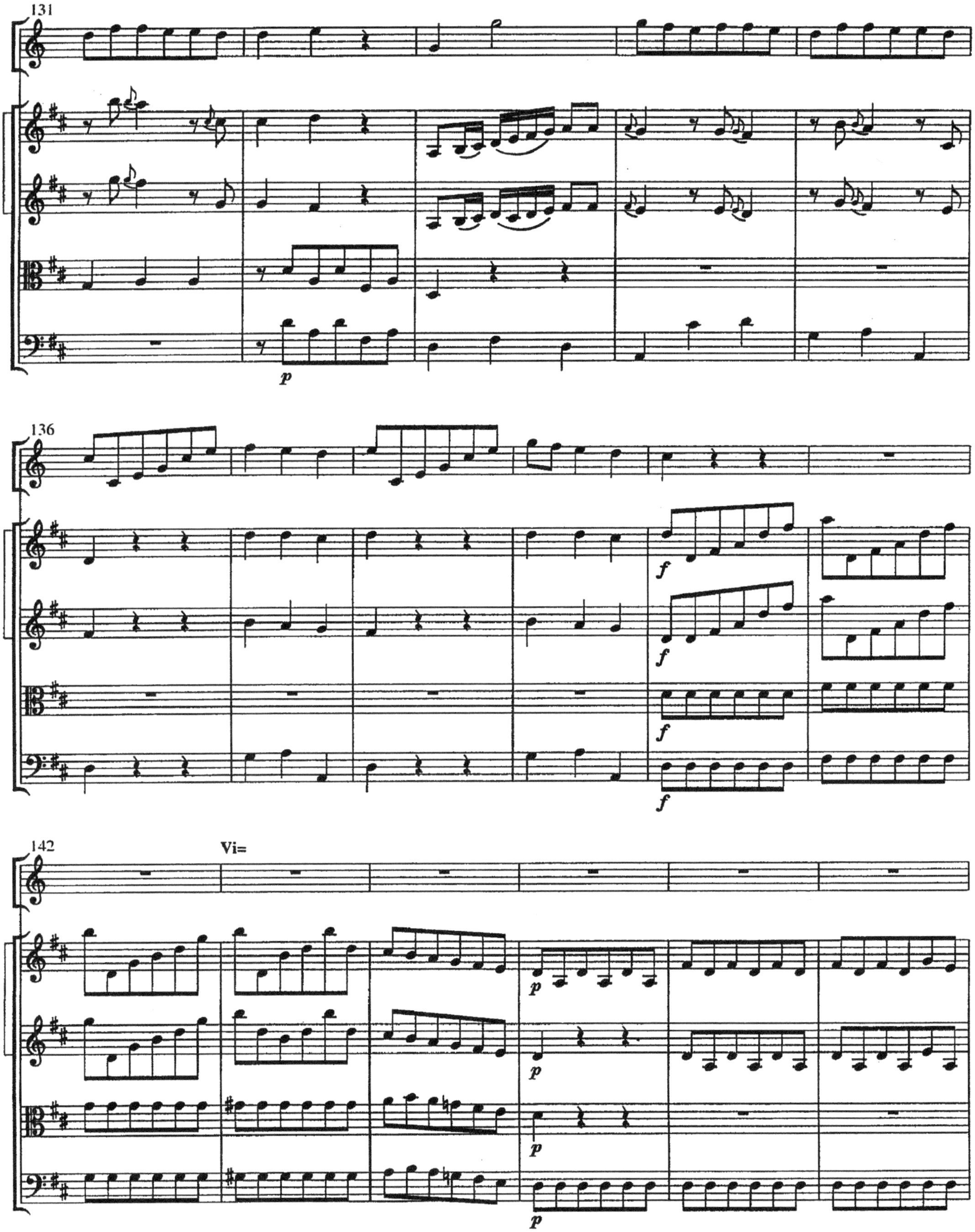
131
p
136
f
f
f
f
142
Vi=
p
p
p
p

* Play notes in small type if cut is used.

76